Do You Really Need A J.O.B?

Reasons Why I Don't Think So and What You Can Do About It

By, Ejeke, P.C

https://www.easyimreviews.com/

Your Exclusive Free Gift

As a way of saying thank you for purchasing and reading this, am offering to give you my next book for free. You will get to be among the first people to get their hands on my next title coming out soon. It is exclusively for all the people that took the time to buy and read this book. In that book, I will be going into greater detail on how you can build a system that generates your passive income year after year even if you are just starting out.

More importantly, it delves into the right kind of mind see that you need to achieve your goals. Whether you realize it or not, you mind set plays a big role in the way you perceive yourself and how you perceive yourself determines just how far and how much money you are giving yourself the chance to make. All you have to do is go to this link and put your name and e-mail and I will send you all the details and get you informed when the book hits the shelves.

Apart from all that, I will be sending you all the information I have on the things I promised in the book, where to get-

1- The book that got me started in kindle publishing; the material is simple, and direct to the point, no fluff and no BS.

2- Free Hosting to any number of sites you want, 1, 2, or heck a hundred websites all for free

3- Free readymade websites for your business or for building your list

4- And all the tools that I use in building my web business, like tools I use for Link Building, Keyword Research, and my List Building tool of choice and of course the book that got me started in kindle publishing, all for free. All you need do is go here now-

https://www.easyimreviews.com/resources/

TABLE OF CONTENTS

Do You Really Need A J.O.B.?

Reasons Why I Don't Think So and What You Can Do About It

By Ejeke, P. C

CHAPTER ONE: DO YOU REALLY NEED A J.O.B.?

CHAPTER TWO: REASONS WHY I DON'T THINK SO

   1 - Security

   2 - Taxes

   3 - Modern Slavery

   4 - Home

   5 - Getting Paid

   6 - You Get No Bonus for Messing Up

   7 - Income Flexibility

   8 - Pajamas

   9 - Focusing on Your Weaknesses

   10 - Negative Working Environment

   11 - Not Because Everyone Thinks So

   12 - Nobody Cares How Many Hours You Work

   13 - Infinite Returns

   14 - Limited Experience

   15 - Inheritance

CHAPTER THREE: WHAT YOU CAN DO ABOUT IT

CHAPTER FOUR: DO YOU HAVE ANYTHING AGAINST COMMISSION SALESMEN?

How Does It Actually Work?

Getting Started With Affiliate Marketing

1 – Pick Affiliate Programs that are relevant to your site or you line of business.

2 - Promoting Those Products and Raking In the Sales

Benefits for Retailers

Benefits for Affiliates

Common Concerns

CHAPTER FIVE: HAVE YOU GOT ANY SSCRAPSS PLEASE?

Step 1 - Take Stock

Step 2 - Set up your EBay Account

Step 3 - Decide how you are going to accept payment

Step 4 - Build up your account

Step 5 - Decide what you want to sell

Step 6 - Space

Step 7 - Find out what you can't sell

Step 8 - What's hot right now

Step 9 - Get all the information you need

Step 10 - Take Good Quality Pictures

Step 11 - The Listing

Step 12 - Respond to Buyers

Step 13 - Ship Your Item

CHAPTER SIX: SO WHO WANTS TO BE THE HUMAN COMPONENT OF A COMPUTER APPLICATION?

CHAPTER SEVEN: DO YOU LIKE THE AMAZON (RAIN FOREST)? WELL, I DO.

CHAPTER EIGHT: BACK FLIPS CAN BE FUN!

Step 1 - Find the Domain Names

Step 2 Acquire the Domain Names

Step 3 Sell the Domain Names

Step 4 Transfer the Domain Names

CHAPTER NINE: OLD MAN NEWMARK

A - Attention
I - Interest
D - Desire
A - Action

CHAPTER TEN: MORE ONLINE MONEY MAKING METHODS

Take Surveys
Sell Photographs
Write Articles
Display Advertising
Produce Videos on YouTube
Complete Micro-Jobs
Provide Freelancing Work
Provide Customer Service
Perform Odd Jobs
Provide Typing Skills
Provide Tutoring

CHAPTER ELEVEN: WHAT IS YOUR WHY?

1 - Start at the Very End
2 - What Will You Do If There Is No Chance Of Failure?
3 - Think About Your Heroes, People You Would Love To Meet
4 - What Do You Love To Do?
5 - Ask Yourself, What Is Your True Purpose In Life?

So What Next?

CHAPTER TWELVE: GOING IN DEEP AND BUILDING YOUR SYSTEM

Going Through the Processes
  Step 1 - Find a profitable niche
  Step - 2 Build a List
  Step - 3 Market a Related Product

The Tools

CHAPTER THIRTEEN: BEFORE YOU QUIT YOUR JOB..... FOR PETE'S SAKE!!

And then the spark!

Reality

My Near Mistake

Keep Your Job, But Part Time

CHAPTER FOURTEEN: HOW BADLY DO YOU WANT IT? PAYING THE PRICE

CHAPTER FIFTEEN: AND FINALLY

Once Again, Your Free Gift,

Excerpts from My Book "Virtual Real Estate Investing"

Disclaimer

CHAPTER ONE

DO YOU REALLY NEED A J.O.B.?

"During times of universal deceit, telling the truth becomes a revolutionary act." - George Orwell (An English novelist)

The truth hurts like crazy but like it or not, it is the truth and nothing you do will ever change that. This is an era of global financial change, a change that will prove difficult for some and a golden opportunity for others. It is a time when the idea of a regular pay check should be the furthest thing on your mind. This is a time that we need not be J.O.B. seekers but capitalists and entrepreneurs.

It has never been any easier then it is now to start a business of your own and don't let me start on all the news about so many teenage millionaires: kids who made and are still making millions even before they are out of college. By the way, if I may ask, what's the big deal about getting a J.O.B.? In case you don't know that word stands for: "Just Over Broke".

M. Raymond summed it up perfectly when he wrote,

> *"We ordinary men lead such lives of routine and seeming meaninglessness that we shun with something like terror any close scrutiny of what we are doing with our years. We awake today and hurry to work as we did yesterday and the day before. Tomorrow it will be the same story. Our work never changes essen-*

> *tially. We are always at the same machine, desk, or chair; always using the same instruments or tools. After a morning of labor, we dash to lunch. Then back to the same routine until the whistle blows or the bell rings. Then we hurry home to an evening meal, read the paper, and go to bed. Tomorrow will be no different."*

If that is not living a zombie kind of life style, I don't know what is. There is no fun, and there is no creativity, which is one, if not the most important, of a human's attributes. Creativity is one thing that sets us apart as humans from every other living thing but when that is lost, when we decide to sacrifice that gift, than we have downgraded ourselves to sub-human status.

According to J. Maurus, in his book **"Make the Most of Your Time"**,

> *Creativity can revivify our society and help to stem the seemingly inexorable match toward the automation of human beings and the steady loss of that freedom which is man's distinctive attribute.*

Truer words have never been spoken.

Times have changed; people are losing their jobs like there is no tomorrow. Companies are finding it more and more difficult to pay pensions. Think about it: has there ever been any time in the history of mankind when the global economy has been this bad? Unemployment rates are at record highs in virtually every country in the world, the middle class is being wiped out, the rich are getting richer by the minute, and the thing is it will get worse before it gets better.

Can you imagine actually working because "you want to" not because "you have to"? These are two different concepts and if you can get this around your head believe me you will begin to see the world differently.

Why would any one control another's means of livelihood? It doesn't make sense to me. The time when the creed was "Go to school, get a good safe and secure job, and save for retirement" is gone. This is the information age: an age when anyone from anywhere can gain access to information literally at the click of a button. This is the time when there is no middle man and no one telling you it can't be done. This is a period in history when you can write a movie script and get a movie made or your book can sell millions of copies with just the click of a button. Just check out the social network revolution: never before have so many people been able to connect in such a manner in the entire existence of the human race. People can interact and exchange ideas in milliseconds and wealth and riches can be transferred from one individual to another, from one part of the globe to another, at the click of a button.

Robert Kiyosaki in his book *Rich Dad's Guide to Becoming Rich without Cutting up Your Credit Cards*, said...

> *"...in 1989, when the Berlin wall came down and the World Wide Web went up, the Industrial Age ended and the Information Age officially began."*

He continued to explain by illustrating with the following table.

1989

Industrial Age	Information Age
Job security	Financial security
Job for life	Free agents
One profession	Many professions
Defined benefit pension plans (employer responsible)	Defined contribution pension plans -401(K) (employee responsible)
Social security certain	Social security uncertain

Medicare certain	Medicare uncertain
Seniority an asset	Seniority a liability
Pay raises based upon tenure	Pay raises a liability since many employers are looking for younger workers with more current technical skills willing to work for less

Looking at the table prior to 1989, you will notice what was possible and important to employees and what parents wanted for their children such as job security, defined benefit pension plans, social security, Medicare, and on and on. The truth is, back then if you were not pursuing those things, you would lose everything and be left behind. The same applies to today since the coming of the internet and the information age: things have changed. Those things are no longer necessary to your survival and financial security. On the other side of the table, you will see the things that the information age brought with it. Those are the things you should try to avoid at all costs now, things that you need to find a way of making sure will not catch up with you in the years ahead, except for "financial security and being a free agent".

Frankly, there is no excuse to not pulling your own weight and getting into the game, a game where you decide for yourself how much money you want and how to get it. All that is required of you is to get off your butt and go to work. Not the J.O.B. but go to work to learn all that is necessary to stay out of the rat race and be able to write your own check.

CHAPTER TWO

REASONS WHY I DON'T THINK SO

Choose a job you love, and you will never have to work a day in your life - Confucius. (A Chinese Philosopher)

Okay, let me break it down for you and give you even more reasons that are close to home why it actually sucks to have the J.O.B. mentality.

1 - Security

Most people think that when they have a job they will be safe and secure. Yes of course it is called a safe, secure job but how safe is it really? Just like everything else in life, there is a price to pay. In my opinion, the price of getting a safe secure J.O.B. is your freedom. If that company goes under, tell me how safe you will feel. What happens when the new manager decides he hates your guts? What then?

There is also the ever changing face of global commerce which can make it difficult for most companies to retain their work force. This, granted, is no fault of theirs but the changes in market forces leave them no choice but to lay off worker after worker. But when you create your own business, there will always be customers to serve: when one customer goes, there will be the next one in line as long as your business remains relevant.

How is it even possible to have security when you don't have control? Employees are the people that have the least control over how much they earn, how they are able earn that much, and indeed their entire lives. Being an employee is another name for a professional gambler. Everything about your life is on the line, and you have no ace up your sleeve.

2 - Taxes

When you get a job, you are likely to pay higher taxes than the guy who employed you. The laws are written to favor them not you, the employee. Worst of all, you are taxed first and whatever is left becomes yours. But your employer spends first and gets taxed on whatever is left. That means if he can legally prove that he only has just a penny left after all business expenses then the government will tax only the penny that is left. A good tax strategist can help you expand the cash within your business without getting you into trouble.

3 - Modern Slavery

Think about it: most people think they work for just eight to ten hours a day but in reality you work more than that. When you get home and you are through with your evening meal or you come back from a night out with your buddies try sleeping late when it's not the weekend; see what happens to you in the morning when you get to work. The truth is that instead of just having fun with your friends, you are busy looking at the time because you need to get back home and get some sleep so you don't get up late in the morning and be late to work. So invariably your boss is still controlling you even when it's not your working hours.

4 - Home

People think buying a house to live in is an investment. It's the same advice: "Son, go to school, get a safe secure job, get married, and then buy a house because the kids will soon start coming". I have never heard of anything so dull, so boring. Just because your job made it possible for you to qualify for a mortgage for your house doesn't make it an asset. Your house could be an asset if someone else is paying for it, and you have a good positive income from it.

You don't need a job to be able to qualify for a mortgage; all you need are good business skills, not job skills, and a proven track record. Yes, you heard me: business skills and a good track record get you a mortgage. So go get a house and rent it out for higher than your monthly mortgage and voila you have an asset and you are in business; it's that simple.

> *"If you want something, find out the price, then pay the price....... But always remember, everything has a price. And the price for becoming rich by being cheap is that you are still cheap" - Robert Kiyosaki*

5 - Getting Paid

When you have a job, you are paid by the hour so the moment you stop working, your money stops coming as well. We have been brain washed into believing that all we need is a steady paycheck but guess what? You still write your own steady paycheck that is more rewarding than your day J.O.B. if you create your own business and build on it by providing value to people every single day.

6 - You Get No Bonus for Messing Up

If you have a job and you make mistakes, you are punished by a pay cut or even a full suspension. Then you have to run around "kissing ass" just to make sure that a much younger co-worker is not promoted over you or even worse that you are not fired. But if you have your own business, when you make mistakes, though painful, you learn one more way not to do business. It's on the job training, and you get better at it as times goes on. Best of all, it's all fun.

7 - Income Flexibility

When you are stuck in a job, it doesn't matter what value you provide, you can only ask for a pay raise and that, too, is a fixed sum as far as the board is concerned. But, in your own business, you only need to open your eyes or get someone to point out to you the different ways you can generate income from the same business you've been doing for years. The possibilities are endless when you take a moment to think about it. You learn to stop thinking in terms of an hourly pay check and start thinking in passive income terms.

8 - Pajamas

Okay, how about working in your home office in your pajamas? You are as comfortable as you want, and there are no limits to your creativity. If you have a job, there will always be that stiff dress code and rules that restrict imagination and creativity to some point. What about the pantyhose for the ladies? How many ladies actually feel comfortable in those things?

As I write this, I am in my boxer shorts sitting on the balcony, laptop on my lap, my feet propped up on the table, a glass of tequila by my side, with the wind gently fanning my cheeks as the birds sing in a nearby tree. Just tell me: how many people get to enjoy a morning like that with some peace and quiet and your creative juices running wild?

9 - Focusing on Your Weaknesses

In the J.O.B. arena, you must have heard of what is commonly referred to as the "360". This is when you are facing a panel that gets to dissect, critic, and judge you regarding your weaknesses. It's not just the panel or your supervisor but also your coworkers with their "holier than thou" attitude who get to analyze your job performance and hand you unsolicited advice while at the same time outlining your weaknesses and telling you the steps that you should follow in order to address them.

But if you are running your own business, you don't have to mess around with your weaknesses or waste valuable resources and, most importantly, your time struggling to try and strengthen your weaknesses. You can simply outsource your weaknesses or hire people to perform those tasks that you are weak in so that you can focus all of your energy and time building on your strengths.

10 - Negative Working Environment

In many instances, the office environment is not always conducive for long term peak performance nor do many offices encourage creative thinking. There is the ever present silent rivalry between co-workers, just under the surface, who are seeking all the attention and good will of the manager, supervisor, or the boss. In your own business, you get to choose who you work with and if you don't like somebody, you simply walk away from that particular deal. You are responsible for all aspects and performance of your business. Granted, this is easier said than done as it can be easier and more comfortable for you to sit back and blame the next person, but you will get to have your freedom on your own terms.

According to Steve Pavlina,

> *"...when you run into an idiot in the entrepreneurial world, you can turn around and head the other way. When you run into an idiot in the corporate world, you have to turn around and say "Sorry, boss".*

11 - Not Because Everyone Thinks So

The worst thing you can do is go get a job just because everyone thinks it's the right thing to do. They don't care if you will be happy living that kind of lifestyle. You need to realize that just because everyone is doing it doesn't make it a good idea or the best thing for you. There are far better ways to make a living than selling your time and yourself to indentured servitude.

12 - Nobody Cares How Many Hours You Work

It's only when you are an employee that you and your employer will ever care how many hours you work. The percentage of people that really care is very small compared to those that don't. For example, how long do you think it took me to write this? Would you pay me twice as much if it took me 3 hours to write this versus 3 days? Most people only care about the value you bring to the table. How much you make depends on the quality of the value you create. Create something of high value, and people will gladly pull out their wallets and offer you money. The best part is if you do it right that creation of yours will be making you money indefinitely. Talk about infinite returns!

13 - Infinite Returns

When you create something of value while working for someone else, your employer gets all the benefits from what you created and you are given a wrist watch as an award. But if you create something within your business, you get paid for years to come or as long as whatever you created remains valuable.

You can do better by building a system. This you can achieve by starting a business such as building websites, becoming an investor, or you can start generating royalty-based income from your creative works like painting, creating songs, or writing books. You name it. The system delivers value to people day after day continuously while generating income for you. So long as it is in motion, it requires little or no tending to. Then you can spend the rest of you time enjoying watching your kids grow or you can use the time to refine that system, tweak it to make it better, and even build more systems versus just maintaining your current income.

14 - Limited Experience

I wonder what good the experience you get from your J.O.B. will do for you outside of your J.O.B. environment. The experience you get on the J.O.B. is on the J.O.B. experience and nothing more. You get experience living you life regardless of whether you have a J.O.B. or not.

The worst thing about getting experience from your J.O.B. is that you usually just repeat the same limited experience over and over again. At first, you learn a lot when you are employed; then you stagnate because there is no next level. Again: if your limited skill set ever becomes obsolete, that experience will be worth shit, and you can kiss that J.O.B. goodbye. Think about it: will your J.O.B. even exist in the next 10 years not to mention your experience on the J.O.B.? But if you are running a business, you learn to deal with the different kinds of people you meet on a daily basis as well as how to respond to and handle different situations and emergencies. These skills you learn will stay with you for as long as you live, and you will continue to use them even outside of your business.

15 - Inheritance

Yea, I bet you never thought of that. It doesn't matter how much value you add to your J.O.B., you can never pass it on to your kids. In fact, the moment you drop dead, your employer will already be looking for your replacement. In your J.O.B., you are simply helping your boss build a legacy for his own kids. But if you have a business of your own, you can easily pass the business on to your kids. This is how legacies are built and passed on from generation to generation.

CHAPTER THREE

WHAT YOU CAN DO ABOUT IT

You could be the light of the world, but no one will know it unless the switch is turned on - John Mason (Author)

There is no better way to secure for your and your family's future except through financial security and true financial security can only be secured when you are in control of how much you end up with in your pocket at the end of every month. In order to do that, you need to **build a business of your own**. With a business, you are in total control of you finances. This is where most people stop dead in their tracks. Building a business, in their own minds, is not easy and doesn't come cheap either. Of course, that is true especially if you don't know what you are doing. You need to first learn what it takes to run a business and be responsible for all of your employees.

That's where the internet comes in. With the internet, you can provide for you and your family while still learning all you need to know about building and running a business. Below are the different types of activities that you can get involved with while learning all about business skills. Everything that I have outlined below has all the elements and structure of a full blown business venture. The same skills that you need to do well selling and marketing on the internet are the same skills you need to run a multi business, on line or off line, only on a larger scale.

CHAPTER FOUR

DO YOU HAVE ANYTHING AGAINST COMMISSION SALESMEN?

"Everyone lives by selling something." ~Robert Louis Stevenson (Author of Treasure Island)

Yes, commission salesmen: that's what I call them. I mean **affiliate marketers**. Ooops!! That probably came out the wrong way, right? Yeah it did, but there is nothing wrong with that. There is nothing wrong with being a salesman/affiliate marketer. On the contrary, you should welcome it. Do you know why? Because you are one already! Before you got married (if you are) you must have sold yourself to your spouse. You will need to show him or her that you are worth spending the rest of his or her life with you. In your office (if you are still on the J.O.B.) you will need to be selling yourself constantly everyday to your boss to prove that you are still relevant to the company. In fact, in all areas of life there is some form of selling involved; it might not be too obvious to you but one way or another we all are selling something from time to time. So for anyone who says, "I don't want to be a salesman" well sorry because you already are so why not relax and enjoy it? Use those abilities and make them pay by applying them in internet marketing.

Affiliate marketing is when you sell someone else a product or a service and collect a commission. I like to use the acronym 'SOPS' (Selling Other People's Stuff). That's simply what it is and nothing more. But actually doing it is something else entirely.

Now let's stretch it a little tiny bit.

Wikipedia defines affiliate marketing as, "A marketing practice in which a business rewards one or more affiliates for each visitor or customer brought about by the affiliate's own marketing efforts."

And if you stretch the definition a bit more, you can describe affiliate marketing as a revenue-sharing plan between a product owner and a would-be affiliate marketer, in this case: **you**, the salesman. This could happen online or offline. In the online arena, an online automated marketing program lets webmasters place advertisements, banners, or buttons linking to the company's products or services on their websites so when a customer buys stuff through that particular website, the webmaster gets a commission.

HOW DOES IT ACTUALLY WORK?

All affiliate marketing does not work in the same way or pay the same way or even pay the same amount. Some of the companies will only enable you to place text or image hyperlinks to products or a website; others will allow you to set up a shopping page or store page that offers products related to the content of your website; and others will only require you to place simple advertising banners or buttons.

Now when it comes to payouts, just as the method of sales and conversions differ, so does the method of payouts. But the most common ways an affiliate is paid are by the following:

1. Paid per click. Each time a person clicks the ad; generally known as pay-per-click advertising.
2. You may be paid a commission when a sale is made; also known as pay-per-sale advertising.
3. You might be paid by lead equally known as pay-per-lead advertising.

Depending on the agreement, affiliates can earn commission each time a visitor clicks the ad, registers for more information, or completes an online purchase, for example. Commissions can vary depending on the nature of the transaction. Retailers generally pay a higher commission for transactions that result in sales as opposed to page views or completed surveys. Commissions are usually paid as either a percentage of the sale or as a flat fixed price.

This way, you will notice that both the advertiser and the webmaster or publisher benefit. At the end of the day, advertisers get more sales of their product when many publishers (or affiliates) promote their product and affiliates. In turn, they will be rewarded with increased revenue by promoting the product. But again, an advertiser pays only when a sale is made, so there is no risk of getting non-converting visits like in some PPC campaigns. That's why most companies make sure that they provide affiliate programs: so they will make more sales through the help of affiliates thus freeing time for them to either create more products or concentrate on perfecting the already existing products to make it much better for the end users.

Most companies will provide full-fledged affiliate pages on their websites so when you sign up, you can get HTML codes to place on your websites. On that same page, you will be able to check your sales statistics. The codes work with a combination of cookies and unique user IDs to track sales or leads and subsequent revenue, as the case maybe. In the case of pay-per-sale, the customer must make a purchase before the cookies expire. Some cookies can be stored on your computer for up to a month while others can be stored up to a couple of weeks depending on the company involved.

GETTING STARTED WITH AFFILIATE MARKETING

When you decide to get involved with affiliate marketing, there are some things that you need to have at your fingertips. In fact, there are two basic things:

1. You must find the right kind of affiliate product to promote.
2. You must also have ready buyers to buy those products.

Most people make the mistake of thinking that as long as the product exists then there must be buyers, right? Well, wrong. The owner of the product could simply have done a very bad job of researching the availability of the market before production so when you join you inherit the same problem as well. Or the product could simply be bad, and who wants to buy a bad product? Therefore, these two points are very crucial to the success of any affiliate; they are 'key' to be precise. Get either one wrong, and you can kiss your commissions good bye.

The following are some tips that might help you get started with affiliate marketing.

1 – Pick Affiliate Programs that are relevant to your site or you line of business.

There is nothing as bad as a visitor coming to a site about elementary school math only to see adverts about online casinos. Therefore, if your site is about travelling then you are better off with affiliate programs that might be advertising airline flight tickets and discounts.

To pick good affiliate programs, you need to:

- **Browse affiliate networks**. These are companies

that are the middle men between affiliates and the companies with products that they need promoted. There are many affiliate networks. The following are my favorites:
- http://clickbank.com
- Commission Junction (aka CJ)
- ShareaSale

- **You can also do a simple Google search.** To do this you can simply type: "your keyword + Affiliate Program" (Replace "your Keyword" with your niche like "Weight Loss Affiliate Programs") and you will easily find the appropriate product to promote.
- **Take a look at online stores.** Online stores like eBay and Amazon all have affiliate programs. You can get accounts with any one of them and promote the products they have listed on their websites.
- **You can check out your competitor.** Exactly: You can take a look at what your competitors are doing and copy them as long as they see success. Better still, copy what they are doing and find a way to make it better, do it better, or add more value to it; that way you can be ahead of them.

2 - Promoting Those Products and Raking In the Sales

Now that we have the products that we want, the next thing is actually promoting those products. There are tons of ways to promote these products but here are some very effective ways to do that:

A. **You Can Use A Blog.** If you own a blog and you have a vibrant community, then you can place related banners of affiliate products on your site or you can write and publish a full review of the product on your site. But remember: your site is your brand so be careful when you promote related products.

B. **Social Networks**. Social networks are big hits when it comes to selling stuff online. To some people, they just concentrate only on social networks without bothering themselves with other promotional channels. The best part is it's free: you don't have to pay a dime. The most popular social networks are Facebook and Twitter.

C. **You Can Submit Related Articles**. You can write and submit related articles about the products that you are promoting. This is called article marketing. You can write the articles yourself or get any good freelancer to write them for you and then submit them to article directories with your affiliate links placed within the article resource box. You do need to know, however, that most article directories do not allow affiliate links in the resource box so your best bet is to write a review of it on your blog then place a link back to the review page on your blog. There are lots of article directories but here are just a few to start with:
- Ezinearticle.com
- Goarticles.com
- ArticleAlley.com
- Ideamarketers.com
- buzzle.com

Article marketing can really be a pain. I personally use ezarticlelinks to build links back to any website or page that I want through article marketing.

D. **Create Videos**. You can equally record videos of you reviewing any product and upload them to YouTube. This has come to be more effective than ever before. With just one video, you can get a ton of traffic to your preferred webpage or site easily and quickly. Make sure you add your affiliate link to the description field for the video and see it go viral in a matter of hours. I don't need to stress the fact that you also have to provide your video with a very catchy caption: this will draw people out and make them click and watch your videos.

E. **Use a web 2.0 site**. I don't know if you have heard of web 2.0 sites. These are like article directories, but there are vibrant communities that are backing them. Here when you place articles related to your affiliate products on sites like Sqidoo or Hubpages, other members can comment on your articles as well as like or dislike them. You need to know that the search engines love these kinds of sites so your articles can rank quickly.

F. **Go To Forums**. Forums are also very popular when you are trying to promote affiliate products. You need to first find a good and highly popular forum, then create an account, and finally on your signature add your affiliate links. That way, when you make a comment on any topic, your affiliate links are always visible to the entire forum members.

G. **Build Niche Sites**. Yes, you can use niche sites to promote your affiliate products. These are highly targeted web pages that are specifically built just for one thing or product, such as a keyword or a niche. They are easy to build, easy to rank, and generally highly profitable when built around a very good and high end product. These kinds of sites don't need lots of pages, just 5 to 10 pages will do. What you have to do is research for a lucrative "Low Competition", "High Traffic" keyword using some keyword tools and then create a website/blog around that keyword and a few related ones. The next step is to start building back links to those pages. In no time, you will rank for your chosen key words. Once that happens, place related banners and affiliate links on them and watch the dollars role in.

Benefits for Retailers

Retailers who are not web savvy or don't have a lot of time to invest in online promotions can outsource their promotion activity to take advantage of expanded audiences that affiliate marketing offers. Affiliate marketing is also popular among retailers with tight advertising budgets because you can tailor your affiliate agreement to only pay for the promotions that result in sales.

Benefits for Affiliates

Webmasters who are looking to earn some extra income find that affiliate marketing offers them the opportunity to make money online without a lot of extra effort, since their websites are already up and running. Affiliates who earn their primary income off marketing tend to spend much more time both researching new partnership opportunities and making their sites more desirable to potential advertisers usually by increasing site traffic and building a good online reputation.

Common Concerns

While it sounds easy, affiliate marketing is not a guaranteed success for retailers or affiliates nor is affiliate marketing for everybody. As affiliate marketing has become more popular over the last few years, websites have become oversaturated with ads. Successful affiliate and retailer relationships are more likely to be found in relevant partnerships where visitors trust both the product and the site where they view the ads.

Affiliate marketing online is a fairly new practice so industry standards and regulations are not fully established. Recently, though, the Federal Trade Commission enacted new rules for affiliates regarding solicitations obtained through transactions, credit reports, or third-party sources. Currently, certifications and training resources are mostly offered on personal or commercial websites specializing in e-commerce activities. Whatever you decide to do, or however you decide to get into making money online, just remember: nothing beats getting started.

CHAPTER FIVE

HAVE YOU GOT ANY SSCRAPSS PLEASE?

> **I have a definite talent for convincing people to try something new. I am a good salesman. When I am on form, I can sell anything. –Brian Eno (English Musician)**

I bet you didn't see that coming. Yes, you can sell your sscrapss on eBay, and you will be surprised what people will be willing to pay you for your sscrapss.

Now that doesn't mean you should sell scraps. Okay, don't get confused here. Your scraps could be something in good working condition that you probably bought by mistake (during one of those impulse buy moments) or something that you do not need at home anymore. These items, on the other hand, will be worth a lot in some other guy's eyes or he might just be a very good collector. You know there are people who just love collecting scraps. (By the way, those scraps items sometimes are worth millions.)

Now before you go further, it's a known fact that when people are starting out on something in which they don't necessarily have a clue on how to do it, they unconsciously manufacture excuses. Excuses like:

"I don't have any scraps in my house."

"No one will want to buy my scraps."

"I am a busy guy; I don't have time to learn how to sell scraps on

eBay."

But I tell you, no matter how clean, tidy, rich, or poor you are there is something in your house or in your garage that you can sell. All you've got to do is just look around and take stock of all you own; you will be surprised that there is stuff that you don't want anymore. Old bicycles, shoes, books, cloths, and so on are some items you can start with. You will also be pleasantly surprised that people in Australia or Canada will want to buy that figurine or those old school record albums.

So how exactly do you go about selling your scraps on eBay?

EBay is a place where you can sell things just like any other market place. It doesn't have the usual barriers to entry such as cost and, again, you have unhindered access to the whole world unlike normal traditional market places where you can only connect with just a few hundred people, usually within your local area.

The following steps will guide you on how to start selling on eBay.

STEP 1 - TAKE STOCK

Look around your house for items that you might want to sell. Look into your garage, your store, your kitchen, and every other place you can think of. Actually, it's best if you go over every space in your house one after the other so you don't miss anything. Again, do not just think only in terms of clothes. What about appliances, tools, all types of equipment, toys, books, craft items, sporting equipment, etc.? You can organize them into categories such as small handy items, medium, large, extra-large, and heavy items. Or you can categorize them according to price range.

STEP 2 - SET UP YOUR EBAY ACCOUNT

Setting up an eBay account is very easy. Just go to eBay.com under your country and register. It is very easy and it's free. After filling out the forms and clicking **register**, you will need to login to the e-mail account you used to register your account and confirm your registration. After that, you are good to go.

STEP 3 - DECIDE HOW YOU ARE GOING TO ACCEPT PAYMENT

After setting up your account, you then need to sit down and decide how to accept payment. This will vary depending on in which country you reside. This will require you to do a little research. Some people might like PayPal; others might want direct deposit into their bank account; while some will prefer to be sent a check. If you have overseas customers, they might prefer a deferent payment from that which you are operating with within your home country. The basic thing is ease of use as well as fast payment and collection methods.

STEP 4 - BUILD UP YOUR ACCOUNT

After signing up, you don't just jump in and start selling your scraps immediately. You will need to build up your account; that way you will get lots of great feedback. This feedback will give you credibility. Once you have credibility, people will trust and respect you and will buy from you. You can build up your account by buying stuff yourself as well as getting involved in the vibrant community; that way, you will have buyers who will trust you and who will buy from you.

STEP 5 - DECIDE WHAT YOU WANT TO SELL

You have to think and decide if you will sell used items or new items. However, selling new items means you have to make a small investment in buying the items you are going to sell. You can get new items in bulk from warehouses and wholesalers and resell them for profit individually. For used items, you may encounter more work to find them such as through real life auctions, thrift stores, direct buys from estates, garage sells, evening markets, bazaars, etc. It really depends on the type of person you are and whether or not you enjoy hunting far and wide for things to sell. To some people, it's a lot easier for them to simply sell the scraps lying around in the house.

STEP 6 - SPACE

For those of you who are trying to de-clutter your living rooms or that over stuffed garage, space will not be an issue. But for those of you who are planning on selling new items, the space issue may turn out to be a big nightmare if not handled correctly from the beginning. When you source for new items to sell, you have to be sure that you have enough space in which to store those items. It's not just about room for storing those items but you also will need a room for packaging and wrapping the items in preparation for shipping.

STEP 7 - FIND OUT WHAT YOU CAN'T SELL

EBay doesn't allow certain items to be sold through their site. Some items are very obvious and some are not so obvious. To find out what you can't sell, drop a note to their help desk.

STEP 8 - WHAT'S HOT RIGHT NOW

You need to do a little research and find out what is hot in the market: what do buyers want to get their hands on desperately? Do a little research. Now this will be a good angle for anybody who is into new items. But for those selling their scraps, this might not really help.

STEP 9 - GET ALL THE INFORMATION YOU NEED

For a good and clear listing, you will need to have certain information handy: information such as weight and length. Then you will also need to weigh and measure the item to better estimate shipping costs.

To properly list your items, you will need the following information:

- item names and similar names
- Brand names
- Model names or numbers
- Sizes
- Colors
- Men's, women's, or children's
- Material
- Etc.

STEP 10 - TAKE GOOD QUALITY PICTURES

You should get one of those digital cameras and take good pictures. You should use nice backgrounds like plain white walls or a nice polished wooden floor, something that will make your pictures stand out. If possible, take more than one picture and take it from different angles. Some buyers will want to see the item from different angles. I would like that, too. Take close ups if necessary.

STEP 11 - THE LISTING

With the information you have put together, you then do your listing. When doing your listing, be very careful with the title. Try to be as specific as possible that way your item stands out on its own and it is unique. At the time of this writing, if you do a search on eBay for the item 'cup', it will fetch you 20,000 listings. But if you do a search for "light blue ceramic cup', that will get you down to 4000 listings. You can see the difference when you have general titles: your item will be grouped with thousands of different items making it difficult for would-be customers to locate your item.

There are other advanced listing techniques but try as much as possible to keep it simple. It's best to do your listing on Sunday so it kicks in on Monday morning and runs through the week days. Try to avoid all the extra up-sells, especially bold and premium listings that way you will keep the cost associated with the up sell during your listing as low as possible. And of course, check for misspellings on your title as it will drastically affect you sales.

STEP 12 - RESPOND TO BUYERS

Some buyers will want to send you email to clarify things; make sure you respond to every single one of them until you make the sale. You should at least check your emails once a day if not more.

STEP 13 - SHIP YOUR ITEM

Once the sale is made, ship the item as soon as possible that way you also build a good foundation for yourself.

Now all the above was about listing but before you actually get to the point where you become what I call an eBay power seller, you need to earn the right of passage. You need to go through what I call several phases:
1. The amateur phase
2. The intermediate phase
3. The professional phase

The amateur phase is the period when you are just starting out selling scraps from within your house. At this stage, you get to learn how eBay works, get a feel of the selling practices on eBay, learn all that there is to learn, and get ready to get creative.

The intermediate phase is when you run out of scraps in your house to sell and you have built up momentum, so you have got to find a way to keep that momentum going. To do that, you can find nearby garage sells and go search for materials to sell. Also, storage auctions can be a huge source of materials you can sell on eBay. Most times you can obtain such auction items for pennies and turn around and sell those same items for hefty profits on eBay.

The professional phase is when you graduate to selling products that you don't own, touch, or see. Here you become what is known as a Drop Shipper. You can put an ad of a product that a company has to sell on eBay so when someone buys the product from you at retail price plus shipping and handling, you turn around and pay the company the wholesale price and have them ship the product to the buyer; then you keep the difference between the retail price and the wholesale price. Throughout this process, you don't have to see or touch the product although this might pose a bit of a problem when you consider that the wholesale company might ship either the wrong product, a damaged product, or even a substandard product. To get around this, you need to find a reputable and registered wholesale company.

CHAPTER SIX

SO WHO WANTS TO BE THE HUMAN COMPONENT OF A COMPUTER APPLICATION?

Never trust a computer you can't throw out a window. –Steve Wozniak (Co-Founder of Apple Computer)

Apparently, there are more people than you might think who want to be the human component of a computer application. Since 2005, thousands of people from over 100 countries around the world have flocked to Amazon CEO Jeff Bezos' brain child, 'Amazon Mechanical Turk', for tasks that they perform and earn some money.

Amazon Mechanical Turk, MTurk for short, was named after a legendary automation that could play chess in the 18th century called "The Turk". Back then, the Turk machine was a real hit as it was reported to have check-mated Benjamin Franklin, a devoted player of the game. It was a wooden man powered by a clock mechanism. The whole thing was one big hoax as it turned out later that a chess grand master was hidden inside the machine and was making all the right moves. (This section is not about the "Turk" but about Amazon MTurk; I just thought you might like to know a little about the "Turk" history.)

MTurk may not be your idea of fun, but it can get you a little money for coffee or some small transport fare. Within the system, Mturk has turned out to be a huge market place were companies have solicited workers to do different kinds of activities like transcribing podcasts for 19 cents a minute or writing blog posts for 40 to 70 cents a word. Turkers, as the community workers call themselves; can also perform tasks or HITS (Human Intelligent Tasks) for which they are paid fees ranging from dollars to single pennies per task (HIT). These tasks could be anything you can think of. You can get tasks that require you to match a color to a photograph, but this same task can confound a computer system. At the end of each HIT, Amazon takes a cut.

In this particular virtual workplace, everything that you see and do in there is on a need-to-know bases; this includes who is doing the work, what the point of the task is, and in most cases the very identity of the company soliciting the work. The folks at Amazon say Mturk provides companies with the chance to tap into what it calls "artificial intelligence". The vice president of product management and development relations for Amazon Web Services, Adam Selipsky, said *"from a philosophical perspective, it's really turning the computing paradigm on its head"*.

Definitely not my cup of tea, but hey, I have personally come across people making some decent money with this system. But I have to tell you: it's most suited for nursing moms and people who have no job at all (at least it's better than nothing) or for people who have lots of time on their hands. With your computer and internet connection, you can willingly become part of a new global workforce: one of the millions of faceless human hands pulling the strings inside a website called Mturk.

Let's say, for instance, you are travelling or waiting for your flight to wherever or you are on the train. To kill time, you might just log on to your Mturk account and kill time by doing a few relatively simple tasks while making money in the process. Lots of people who do this are not in there for the money per say; they are just using their time judiciously. The little money you make can go for little gifts to your kids or relatives.

It's a sort of diversion for some people: a diversion from

the day-to-day grind and stress. I consider it a cross between you wanting to make money online on the side while still engaged in your normal job. You can equally consider it a cool substitute to doing word puzzles; this way you are entertained, and you earn some money along the way. 'The Turkers' have even formed their own online community called Turker Nation. That's to show you just how dedicated people can be even though the pay for performing these hits is relatively low.

The down side to this virtual workplace, though, is that there is no way of guaranteeing that you will be paid for the HITS you've performed. Turkers can still be denied their money even if the work done is top notch. That's just how the system is. The best a worker can hope for is to report the incident to Amazon, and the requester will be banned. There will then be a negative word-of-mouth review spread about the requester giving the requester a bad track record within the Mturk Community. This, in turn, will make it increasingly difficult for that requester to get Turkers to do his or her HITS. But all that won't stop the requester from getting another account with a different identity will it? Probably not but hey, nothing in life is one hundred percent safe, right? You've got to do what you have got to do. Okay, that might not be safe enough. How about the Amazon rain forest?

CHAPTER SEVEN

DO YOU LIKE THE AMAZON (RAIN FOREST)? WELL, I DO.

"We see our customers as invited guests to a party, and we are the hosts. It's our job every day to make every important aspect of the customer experience a little bit better." Jeff Bezos (Founder of Amazon.com)

This could well be one of the oldest and the most proven money making techniques in the entire world: the selling of 'how to' information. These are products that give you information on how to solve certain kinds of problems, teach you to learn how to do certain kinds of things in a variety of subjects, or are simply products that educate people.

Amazon publishing has become the number one place for authors to publish their books and have it delivered to millions of people with just the click of a button. In particular, authors are flocking to Amazon Kindle's book publishing system.

The notion that the world is going digital is no gimmick at all because in 2011, Amazon announced that kindle books sales had exceeded the sales of hardcover books and paperback books combined. I remember some years back when I first watched the review of kindle on a CNN broadcast. The presenter voiced that what consumers wanted was the need for the feel of the real paper, the crisp sound as you flip the pages, and the old reassuring smell of printing paper. Now, we are seeing a massive shift in thinking. More and more people are accessing digital materials on the move, so the Kindle is taking the forefront in the book arena.

In the last quarter of 2012, it was announced that eBook sales rose by as much as 28.1%, according to Mashable.com compared to 2011. Across all the trade publishing, eBook sales saw a record growth of 130% which translates to about two billion dollars. This is a huge opportunity for anybody, whether you are a professional writer or just out to get a slice of the pie for yourself. There is no longer any excuse about not meeting the standards of those big publishing houses. Not only that, technology has made it even easier to get published. So much easier, in fact, that you can get your material written, uploaded to your Amazon account, and someone half a world away can download it digitally in a matter of minutes and be reading it on his or her Kindle or any other e-reader of his or her choice. But as far as I am concerned, Kindle beats all other e-readers hands down any day and any time.

Thanks to the kindle, you can instantly download and read practically any material in a digital format from anywhere around the world that has internet connectivity. Amazon announced last December that customers bought over a million kindle devices per week.

Amazon and its product, the kindle, have helped create huge financial successes stories. These are all over the internet. For instance, there is Amanda Hocking. She was turned down again and again by almost every publishing house she went to until she decided to do it herself. At age 20, she went and self-published her "Trylle Trilogy" series on Amazon and sold over 500,000 copies. That success netted her a $2 million book deal with St Martin's Press.

Not only that, we have come to the era when a writer takes a bigger chunk off of their book sales unlike a few years back when the publishing houses took the lion's share. With Amazon if you publish a book, you stand the chance of raking in 70% of the profit while the rest goes to Amazon.

They say being in the right place at the right time could be the best thing that will ever happen to you when it comes to business and making money, and Amazon kindle is one of those moments. Sometimes you have to seek out those moments on your own but sometimes, too, they can just literally fall into your laps just like this opportunity of publishing on Amazon has presented itself.

So join in on the game and learn as you go; you don't have to spend years learning before you can get in. There is no franchise like buy-ins. There are no huge start-up costs like other traditional businesses. There is no waiting for five years before you can ascertain if your business will be profitable in the long run. With online publishing, you will know whether you are successful in weeks, not months or years. Best of all, since there is little to no up-front investment, if your business is not successful, you would've lost just a token compared to the kind of money involved in traditional businesses.

Don't forget to do your research, though. This is very important. There is no point in spending all that time, energy, and sweat to put together a product only to discover that no one wants it so be sure to do adequate research. You can begin by going to click bank market place and look for the kind of digital products that have a high gravity score. The higher the gravity score indicates that people are buying that product like crazy. You can also go to google.com/trends and also pulse.eBay.com to see what's selling. With all this information, you can cross reference all of them to come up with a really good idea of what problems people are looking for answers to and what people are buying, so you can create an info product that fills all those vacuums.

And again, all the technology you need is out there and as cheap as can be. All of the resources that will help increase your chances of success online are already at your beck and call. There are the instant payment systems and instant delivery systems putting information marketing at light speed. With just a click, information can be shared all around the world instantly; all you need to do is make the first step: start your business and the rest will be history.

CHAPTER EIGHT

BACK FLIPS CAN BE FUN!

If you are stuck between two options, just flip a coin in the air! It works. Not because it solves the problem ... but because while the coin is in the air, you will get to know what your heart is really hoping for. –Unknown

You can equally make tidy sums of money flipping expired domain names. Now for those of you beginners that don't know what a domain name is, a domain name is the address you type into your search bar that points to your website. It usually starts with a 'www.' and ends in a ".com, .net, .org, or .biz" and so on. There are tons of them. Domain names are bought from registers for a set period of time, usually 1 year or 2 years at a time. An example of a domain name is "**easyimreviews.com**".

You might ask: what is an expired domain name? This is a domain name that the owner failed for some reason to renew after its initial purchase period came to an end. When this happens, that particular domain name becomes available for anybody to buy and build a website around.

Now you may wonder: what's the value in an expired domain that the original owners failed to renew or don't need any more? You see, when the original owner registered that domain name, he or she had plans for it except in some cases some people might buy a domain for just a quick sell of their product and that is all. So if he or she built a site around that domain and promoted it and built back links to it, then this domain will have some traffic still attached to it. That traffic is what makes the expired domain names valuable. So when the new owner buys the domain, he or she will be able to rank in the search engines faster than if he or she was working with a brand new domain. So all you need do is to find these expired domain names and sell them to people that want them for their inbound links and residual traffic still attached to them.

Most of these domains are very inexpensive: around $10, $20, or $50 and you can sell them for $100, $500, or even a thousand dollars depending on how lucky you are to find a really valuable one and how you go about your promotions. There have been people reported to have built multimillion dollar businesses around just finding and selling domain names. Some domain names have been reported to have been sold for thousands and millions of dollars. Will you be lucky enough to find such domains? Maybe! More than likely you won't but with good research you can still find good valuable domains that you can sell for a really good amount of money. You need to bear in mind, though, that not all the domain names you find will sell; you will generally lose money on some, and that is where the Fast Flipping Formula (FFF) comes in. This is a formula developed and made popular by a noted internet marketer, speaker and entrepreneur, Bob Gatchel

With this technique, you can find and sort the domain names in a matter of minutes, and your chance of hitting a home run with a domain name is increased drastically. The Fast Flipping Formula can be done in 4 steps:

STEP 1 - FIND THE DOMAIN NAMES

Here, to find the **best hosting services**, all you do is to find the domain name. You go about this like you are mining for gold: you need to sift through the dirt and rubbish to find the gems buried deep inside. The best place you can find these domain names are at a website called networksolutions.com. When doing your search, you will need to arm yourself with the right keywords that are related to the niche you want to market; otherwise, you will be flooded with thousands of domain names, making sorting through them hell on earth. So with these five or seven keywords, you can put them into the network solutions search box and push the search button, and you will be presented with a few hundred domain names which you can then easily go through.

But before doing that, you need to bear in mind that there are four key criteria that you need to follow in order to be able to do your sorting and sifting accurately. These four criteria are:

1. The domain names must not contain numbers, e.g. 123stomachabs.com. These are generally useless; people put the numbers when they can't get "stomachabs.com".
2. The domain names must not contain hyphens, e.g., stomach-abs.com. Again, these kinds of domain names are cheap and do not sell very well in the market.
3. The domain name must not exceed 24 characters in length. The shorter the better and the more valuable it will be. This helps to prevent spelling errors when people are conducting a search, it is easy to remember, and will not cause typing fatigue.
4. The domain name must end in a ".com" only, no

".net", ".org", etc. These are generally not valuable and won't sell in the market place.

So with all of that criteria entered into the network solutions search system, you can push the **search** button, and the system will present to you hundreds of domain names. Next, all you need to do is cut and paste these domain names into a text file. Then, you go to godaddy to see if these domain names are available. This is because the system is not perfect; you can be presented with domain names that are still in use due to a system error. This takes just five seconds on a godaddy bulk search tool and will help to reduce the total number of domain names even further.

Next, you will want to do what I call a sanity check: take a look at those domain names and ask yourself if they stand out to you, do they sing to you, do they make sense, and/or do they have a universal appeal to them? Would any one of them be a domain you would like to use as a website name for your business? This will further reduce the total number to probably 4 or 7 domain names.

Step 2 Acquire the Domain Names
You can just buy the domain names directly from godaddy.

Step 3 Sell the Domain Names
The next thing you do is sell the domain names. You can sell them on eBay. You can set the auction and start the bidding price at any amount you like but check what others are doing so you don't stray far off and be the odd man out. You don't want to price the names too high or too low.

Step 4 Transfer the Domain Names
This stage is very easy: you just pick up the phone, call godaddy, tell them you have sold your domain name, instruct them to initiate the transfer to the new owner, and that's it.

CHAPTER NINE

OLD MAN NEWMARK

Don't wait for extraordinary opportunities. Seize common occasions and make them great. Weak men look for opportunities; strong men make them.- Orison Swett Marden (An American Author)

Craigslist.org (CL) is probably one of the most trafficked websites on earth. This is a free add site founded by Craig Newmark. It is a free community where anybody can post an ad for products or services that they are into. Since the early days, the site has grown in leaps and bounds to all the major cities around the world, giving people who advertise there a worldwide reach, fast and instantly. The site doesn't have any fancy graphics on it; in fact, it is (my apologies Mr. Newmark) very ugly and boring with nothing on it but tons of text ads but make no mistake: the site is very powerful since your ad gets seen all around the world. This gives any smart entrepreneurs the opportunity for unlimited income.

Making money on CL can be stripped down to two simple techniques:

1. You can sell your own products or services.
2. You can sell other people's products or services.

Setting up a CL account is very easy. First, just go over to CL, enter your email, and fill out any other forms necessary. This usually takes only minutes, and the system will send you an e-mail just to verify that you are a real person. But when you want to post, they may require phone verification as well. This is no problem: the system calls you to give a four digit code that you can use to do your posting. This is to help make sure that you are not a hacker or spammer using a robot or some other kind of software that is trying to throw up irrelevant ads in the wrong places.

Remember what I said initially: when you want to promote anything be sure to do your research. You can use google.com/trends to find out what people are searching for or the trends that are current. To do this, you use Google's search tool: google.com/trends.

CL is filled with lots of cities. How do you know in which city to post your ads? All you need to do is go to googl.com/trends and enter the website you want to search information for like craigslist.org and the search engine will present you the top ten most trafficked cities on CL. This allows you to know where your target audience is hanging out, and you can find products to promote from click bank, commission junction. and link share. It doesn't matter where you get the information but make sure that it's what people are looking for.

After you have put up your ad, remember to give it a good and catchy headline and then you need to write a little ad content to go with your product link. To do this, I usually use the technique 'AIDA':

A - Attention

Here your headlines will create the attention that you need. You just have to be creative and put up a headline that is eye catching, something that will stop anybody in his or her tracks. Instead of clicking away, the person will pause to take a closer look at your ad.

I - Interest

Now that you have their attention, your next task is to create interest for your service or product within them. You let them know that this is the place that they will get the information that they are searching for or the answers to their problems.

D - Desire

As they are busy reading, you add another level to the whole mix by carefully creating desire by making it clear to them that your service or product is what they really need as well as giving them the reasons why your product or service is what they need to solve whatever problem they have.

A - Action

Then take action: you tell them exactly what they need to do next in order to obtain your product or service. If possible, spell it out for them step by step. Make sure your instructions are to the point and make it clear and easy for them to follow. Do not leave any room for doubt.

These are the four criteria that you need to keep in mind when writing your ad. In addition, you can also upload pictures. This is sure to make your listing stand out and draw more attention. You can also post ads on CL that you can have drop-shipped to your customers.

CHAPTER TEN

MORE ONLINE MONEY MAKING METHODS

"High expectations are the key to everything." - Sam Walton (Founder of Wal-Mart)

The aforementioned are not all of the different ways one can make money online. In fact, there are tons of them: some good, some not so good. I will discuss in this section some other nice methods for you to get your hands wet, get things rolling, and get a feel of what it actually takes to make a dollar online; and then scaling it to tens of thousands of dollars. The following are also just some of the online money methods out there that you might consider as well. Just remember that it takes patience to see any real results, and it's usually something you'll want to start out doing part-time (as the rewards can be small at first) and then build from there. I always tell people to try to make the first dollar and then build on that.

Take Surveys
One way to make money online is to start taking surveys. There are numerous companies that will pay you to take simple surveys. Most surveys won't take very long to fill out, and you can do these in your spare time. The money you gain will be minimal to begin with, but you can get larger payments on occasion as well as rewards and other compensation. Plan to do several surveys before you see any real results.

Sell Photographs

If you are good at taking pictures, there are numerous sites online that will pay you for your photographs. Simply post your photographs on these sites and when someone buys an image, you'll get a royalty. If you have a significant photograph collection, you can make a decent income doing this. Your results will be slow to start out but the more images you provide that are high quality, the faster the income will accumulate.

Write Articles

Many websites, blogs, and magazines require articles online. Article writing is a simple way to begin making money online. You need some decent skills in writing to see any real results from article writing, but there are plenty of jobs out there for you. Plan on making small amounts of money to begin with, but the results down the road can be well worth the initial effort. You may also get noticed by other people who are willing to pay you more for your work.

Display Advertising

If you own a blog or website, you can make money from displaying advertising on the site through sites such as Google AdSense. When someone clicks on an advertisement on your site, you are paid a royalty. Many website owners make a significant income from AdSense. This will only work if your blog or website is already quite established online as you need a great deal of sustained traffic to see any big numbers from AdSense.

Produce Videos on YouTube

Another way to make money online is to produce videos and put them on YouTube. This video content site is one of the largest sites online and gets millions of visitors each day. By placing your videos on this site, you can take advantage of this traffic and make money from the Google advertisements placed on your videos. The more traffic you get, the more money you have the potential to make. Many people make a full-time income with

YouTube as the traffic numbers on the site are staggering.

Complete Micro-Jobs

Many sites such as Fiverr will pay you to do small tasks such as create articles, provide website traffic for someone, or make a video. This site allows you to set the job you want to do and once the task is completed, you get paid for it. This can be an easy way to make money if you have tasks that don't require much time for you to complete. Micro-Job sites don't pay you a whole lot of money, but there's the potential to make more money as you can add extra features to your job for more income per task after you have been on these sites for some time.

Provide Freelancing Work

Another way to make money online is to become a freelancer with whatever skills you have such as writing, website creation, programming knowledge, editing, and so on. Sites such as oDesk and Elance will pay you to do freelancing jobs. All you need to do is bid on a job and if the employer accepts your proposal, you can begin the work and get paid once it is done. If you have good skills, you can make a full-time living on these freelance sites especially if your skills are in high demand.

Provide Customer Service

Online you can make money being a customer service representative for some company. Sites such as workingsolutions.com will hire you to do customer service for them. Your pay will be minimum wage, but you can make a small part-time income doing this if it's something you would like to do. This isn't a job for everyone since you'll have to deal with the public, but it can be something worth doing if you need the money.

Perform Odd Jobs

Through websites such as Twitter and Facebook you might be able to connect with people who need some odd job done such as a blog post, article, or something similar. As long as your skills match what they need, they might consider hiring you for a low fee as it's easier than trying to hire someone in the "real world". Small data entry tasks are an example of odd jobs you can do online.

Provide Typing Skills

If you have blazing fast typing speed, you might find work online typing transcriptions such as medical billing and other work. You can make a decent income doing this type of job; however, some jobs require that you have some type of medical background/knowledge before you can begin typing medical transcriptions, but there are other transcribing jobs available, too, if you look for them.

Provide Tutoring

You might find a job online as a tutor if you have the right skill set. For example if you have skills as a musician, you might tutor students directly online instead of going to a music school. Other tutoring jobs can include regular school classes and other areas such as cooking, health, or Internet marketing. The tutoring job you take will all depend upon your skills.

Those are just some of the examples of jobs online that you can do, and I call them "Skimming the Surface". Don't try to do them all; just pick one and run with it. Most of all, make sure you take action. All of the techniques discussed above can be expanded, enhanced, and turned into great systems if you will just give yourself a chance and try.

Just remember, like I said before, that most of these J.O.B.s will be part-time for the most part but don't get me wrong: it is possible to go full-time as well. But in order to do that, you need to build a really strong system around any one of the J.O.B.s you chose to pursue; otherwise, they will simply become just another kind of J.O.B. for you.

However, having a J.O.B. online as opposed to regular 9-5

J.O.B does not have to be a problem if you can keep your focus and constantly remind yourself that it's only a means to an end. Performing these J.O.B.s will afford you the time you need to learn all of the business skills that you will need when you are ready to launch your own business.

The reason I say part time is, in my own opinion, you can use the free time that you gain by doing these J.O.B.s to learn more about building genuine business systems. I will discuss more about this in the next chapter.

CHAPTER ELEVEN

WHAT IS YOUR WHY?

"It doesn't interest me what you do for a living. I want to know what you ache for, and if you dream of meeting your heart's longing"

-Oriah (Canadian Teacher and Author)

To really have **resounding success** with a business will depend on your reason for wanting to create and build a business in the first place. This reason or your "why" has to come from deep inside you; you have to do the soul searching yourself. It's not something someone can suggest to you but something that will compel you to hold yourself accountable for your eventual success or failure. Do you want to build a business for just the money or do you have a higher purpose for all the toil and hard work? What exactly is your reason for wanting to build a business?

I have given you lots of reasons why you might not like to go look for a J.O.B., but those reasons might not connect with you at all; they might not really make you sit up and do what it takes to actually see your dreams come true. You need to find that reason yourself. It should be your reason and not anyone else's. You need something much stronger: something that will force you to keep going when it seems you have come to the end of the road, something that will make you put in a little extra work when others are fast asleep, and something that should be bigger and stronger than you; it should be your reason why and yours alone.

Believe it or not, money is the bottom line for everything we do in our lives. Or is it really? Sometimes I do ask myself what's the entire struggle for in the first place? Being an Entrepreneur is a cherished way of life for most people and to some others it's something much deeper; it's something that means much more than the money. Which one is it for you? Are you the type that can do just about anything for money or are you the type that sees money as only a means to an end, as just nothing but a tool to get you from one point in life to another? Whichever it is, it's your life, it's your conscience, and you are the one that has to deal with and live with it. It's your decision to look for that reason that pushes you to achieve your goals beyond ordinary women or men. If your life is all about making all the money you can just so you can keep up with the Joneses then what a dreary life that is.

If you have made that choice and you are living the life already, well I guess "it's a free world" right? But, if you are contemplating which road to take, just hang on for a minute and join me: let's analyze this for a while.

There is no doubt about the power of money in our lives; I mean how would the world be without it? Money helps us do lots of things; it makes life easy and worthwhile. There is no point in going into the points of what money can do in our lives. The short of it is that no matter what anybody tells you that they don't care about money, just know that they are just kidding themselves and living in a dream world. One of my mentors, Robert Kiyosaki of the richdadpoordad, once said that you will face problems whether you are rich or not so why not just strive and get the money and enjoy yourself while dealing with the problems in your life? At least you will have the money to cushion the effects of those problems instead of suffering on both angles. Even with no money, you are still going to have your life issues to deal with just like very one else.

But the down side of having money is that you can eat all

the good food you want, drive all the posh cars you want, own all the choice estates all around the world you want but if all of these things are just what you live for then you will be one empty human being. You won't need anyone to tell you that there is something missing in your life, something you just can't quite place your finger on, and believe me it's a real feeling.

So why do we do it any ways? Why do we have to keep building businesses and systems or try making money online and expanding our business interests and holdings instead of just simply going out there and getting a "real" J.O.B? It's all about striking a balance; it's about finding meaningful work that is not "really work' to you, something that you have fun doing that doesn't feel like work while you are doing it; something you can spend 15 to 20 hours working on without feeling like you have done any work at all whenever you feel like it. It has to be something you love, something to look forward to, instead of something you are dreading.

If you ask any online entrepreneur, they will tell you that when they first started out it was all about the money; even me: it has been all about the money and even to some extent right now it still is because one still needs to put food on the table and have a place to sleep, right? But then beyond the money, I have come to realize that the deeper I move into my journey looking for solutions to breaking out of the rat race, the more I reflect on the end point of my journey. Every single day I do that soul searching and every day I come face-to-face with a different facet to my personality. I am beginning to understand that being an entrepreneur is not just about the money; it's a way of life. It's much more than creating businesses and making lots of money. It's about you, your core values, and your outlook about life in general. It's all about making the world a better place to live in for yourself and those around you. Being an entrepreneur is about impacting the world positively with all that you have.

Okay, if you have got your why, and I mean the real reason

deep inside yourself that compels you to seek a different way to make a living other than the J.O.B., then that's good. So, the next thing is: how do you go about finding that something that you love so much, that something that won't seem like work at all while you are working on it? I know how it feels, believe me. I know what it feels like when you dread Monday mornings.

Here are a few ideas and points that I have applied to my life on daily basis and still do to this day. These are things that you need to be working on in your life all of the time: you breathe, sleep, and eat them. You reflect on them while you are taking your bath, taking a dump, cooking breakfast, jogging, or even while you are at work every single day of your life.

1 - Start at the Very End
Picture in your mind's eye what it will be like when you have finally arrived at your life's destination point. What will it be like after you have run all of the race, done all of your work, achieved all you have ever dreamed of, and dusk has set in, and you are about to retire and take a rest, and you cannot physically work anymore? Perhaps after you are dead and gone, what will your loved ones remember you by? What will people remember you for? Just write it all down; be realistic and optimistic and don't overdo it.

2 - What Will You Do If There Is No Chance Of Failure?
Just imagine that there is no chance of you failing at anything. What is that single thing that you would absolutely love to do? This is where you pay attention to your deepest fears and inhibitions and bring them all out in the open and face them squarely head-on. This exercise might not really be the easiest but the earlier you do it, the better. There isn't anyone who doesn't have inhibitions and self-esteem issues; we all do. Even the most accomplished people on earth still have these issues even when they are at the height of their careers. Just do a search

for most of the celebrities that perform on stage and you will learn they still have stage fright each time they are about to go out on stage to perform; then you will understand that having issues is nothing unique to you.

3 - Think About Your Heroes, People You Would Love To Meet

Now, I love this section: think about your heroes and write them down. These are people that have influenced your life in one way or another. They are people that you look up to. They don't have to be famous people; they could just be everyday regular guys on the streets, but they have influenced or affected your life in some way. It could be the way you think or reason. You have to ask yourself what is it that they have achieved that you want to achieve as well. Look for something in their life story that you can relate to or connect with. More often than not, there is always a connection (most likely not directly) between what they have accomplished and/or are doing that you want to accomplish or you are still doing.

4 - What Do You Love To Do?

Okay!! Here we go: I must admit, this is a tough one, even for me. Most people find this a breeze but frankly it's about the most difficult for me. Why? Because some of the things that I love doing I have yet to find a way to turn them around to my favor, but I am seriously working on it. So, here you ask yourself what is it that you love doing? It has to be something that appeals to you, something that while you are doing it you don't notice the time fly by. So the trick is discovering what it is that you love to do and spend more time doing those things and then delegate the rest.

5 - Ask Yourself, What Is Your True Purpose In Life?

Again, take out a sheet of paper and write down your life

goals or purpose. Ask yourself this question several times and each time answer as clearly as you can. As you do this, you will notice that it's not as easy as it sounds but just do it anyways; a little soul searching won't hurt you. Don't just do it twice or three times and then stop; the fact is it might take you a couple of days but just keep doing it until it hits you like a sledge hammer. When you discover it, you will feel a connection to it emotionally; it will be like the scales have fallen off your eyes and then you see the light.

SO WHAT NEXT?

After you have found your purpose, and what you think you should devote your time and your life doing, what then? What's next for you? One basic truth is that not everybody is cut out for the business environment and not everybody can be an entrepreneur. Some people love their jobs; they just love being employees. They simply love the security of a steady paycheck, and you can't argue with that. But for you, who knows? Maybe your gifts will shine more brightly in the business environment. If so, then give it room and let it shine; don't stifle it. You need to find a business model that allows you to do those things that you do best and then delegate the rest of your activities. Of course, you will need to build a team that can work with you. You can also try outsourcing those activities if you like.

Finally, it's not just about the money but all about discovering your true self and building a lifestyle that you love, one that makes you feel fulfilled in all aspects of your life. It's not about lying on the beach all day long, and money will be pouring into your bank account. We are not designed that way; you must do some kind of meaningful work, something that will make you happy and allow you to go to that beach when you want to while still providing value for others and enriching people's lives as well.

CHAPTER TWELVE

GOING IN DEEP AND BUILDING YOUR SYSTEM

"A bad system will beat a good person every time" (W. Edwards Deming, Total Quality Management)

Don't forget, Martin Luther King Jr. said it best. He said, "Everybody can be great because anybody can serve".

After you have found your why, and whatever it is you want to do with your life, then the next thing is to build your character or your mind set if you will. Whether you are just skimming the surface or going in deep to actually create a worthwhile business (whether it is online or it is offline) that will last the test time and set you truly free, there is a certain kind of mind set that is required.

You see, most people when starting out jump straight into how much money they are going to make but before you can think of your pocket, you need to address your head first. You need to have the "Can Do" spirit. You need to first believe within you that yes, you can do it, and you are willing to push on no matter what the setbacks are or what the circumstances are that surround you. You need to have the will power and the mental toughness to push on even if you fail. This is one big reason why so many people fail when trying to start out on their own. They throw up their hands and say, "No, it's not for me" when they are just one more try away from striking gold.

Now when you have got that "Can Do" spirit well-established within your psyche then the next thing most beginners do that you should **avoid** is asking, "How much money can I make?" Now don't get me wrong: I know I said it's not all about the money, and there is nothing wrong in asking that; after all, your primary reason is to make money, right? But it's the wrong question to ask as a beginner. For a beginner, the most important questions you should be asking yourself are:
1. How can I add value to people's lives?
2. How can my business help other people?
3. What problems can my business solve?
4. What solutions can you offer with your business?

All of these questions can be summed up in just one word: VALUE. Simply put: this is all it takes to make money online or even offline for that matter. You need to keep the facts at the tips of your fingers so that you get paid for the value you bring to the market place (LIFE). All you need to do is make yourself more valuable or become more valuable to people, and the money will follow naturally.

This same principle can be discerned from the law of Karma which is the law of cause and effect or as Ralph Waldo Emerson puts it, *"The law of compensation"* which states that "Your income is determined by how many people you serve and how well you serve them".

Now if you look closely at this, you will discover that there are two things that are quite clear here:
1. It means that the level of the pay you get is always under your control because if you want more money, you simply look for more people to serve. The internet has presented us all with a wonderful opportunity to be able to do this relatively easily and cheaply compared to a few years ago.
2. There are also no limitations to what you can earn as you can always find more people to serve.

This is another part where people get it wrong as well so asking yourself the right questions takes most of the frustration and struggle away when you are just starting out.

Now the 64 million dollar question is: can you do it? Do you have what it takes? Can you actually stop thinking about the dollar signs and focus on not just the value but the quality of the value you can bring to the market place? Well, only you can answer that on your own but if you can bring value then be ready to enjoy one of the rare privileges most people find difficult to accomplish.

GOING THROUGH THE PROCESSES

Now that you are sure you have the correct mind set, the next step is for you to address the exact processes that are needed to build a business and eventually make money online.

Someone once said, "Systems work; its people that fail," and you know what? That's absolutely true when you stop for a minute to think about it. Humans fail or give up completely, usually just short of achieving their goals. This happens because of our inherent imperfections and ability to judge and criticize.

Here you can work on creating and perfecting a system that works for you whether you are there or not: you can be sleeping or out jogging, you can be driving the kids to school or having some real quality time with your significant other and the system will generating passive income for you. This system will need to be what you can identify with, one that works for you, and one that can easily fit around the lifestyle you've chosen for yourself.

Now if you've not heard this before and you are just starting out, this will blow you away. Why? Because it's so easy and simple once you get it working correctly. It's the starting point that's always difficult. I learned this from one of my long-time mentors, Chris Farrell; in fact, I am still learning form him as I write this.

Step 1 - Find a profitable niche
This is when you look for a particular market where people are already buying stuff. Now don't get all worked up by asking what you will sell because what you will be selling is the last piece of the puzzle within the whole system. Also, do not worry whether you know anything about that niche or not, though it helps if you do. For now just concentrate on getting the core concepts into your head.

There are three major core markets to choose from and thousands of niches within these markets to choose from. The three major markets are:

1. The Lifestyle Market
2. The Money Market
3. The Health Market

Each of these markets is very broad, and each is a multi-million dollar market. Within each of these markets are other smaller areas called "niches". There are literally thousands of them such as Become A Mystery Shopper, Hiring Virtual Workers, Care Options For Your Elderly Parents, Planning Your Summer Vacation On A Budget, How To Work In Hollywood, Home Schooling, Writing Your Own Book, Become A Better Public Speaker, Yachting, Greenhouse Gardening, Beginners Guide To Yoga, Ideas For A Birthday Party Your Child Will Never Forget, and How To Work On The Radio. They range from Weight Loss to Brides, from Muscle Building to Skinny Men, from How to Become a Pilot to Event Planning, from Time Management Strategies to Cake Decorating and the list just goes on and on and on.

Later I will show where you can get your hands on Already Made Websites for free. Mind you these websites on there will cost you between two to three hundred dollars per piece should you want to design them from scratch.

Step - 2 Build a List

In case you haven't heard, "The money is in the list". That's the slogan that has been popular especially within the internet marketing circles. Believe me, nothing else is as important as building your list. Here you will only be concerned with building a list of subscribers within a particular niche who are interested in that very topic.

What this means is that you build a one page website that contains your copy and 2 boxes for collecting visitors names and e-mail addresses. When this happens, you can then market to them directly via a technique known as e-mail marketing. This will help you to market to those people directly and at any time you feel like it.

This is the single most important thing you can do for your business and again don't worry if you have no idea how to do this. I will be pointing you to a place where I learned how to do mine later on. For now, just concentrate on knowing just how important list building is.

Most people, especially beginners, make the mistake of wanting to focus on a product, but they are at a loss as to what product to market. Some worry about the look of their website but let me tell you right now: products or websites are not businesses. You might ask, if these two are not businesses then what is? Well, your business is your list. You can have a product or have the best looking website but if there is no one to buy your product, how then do you make any money? Having the best looking website won't mean squat if there is no traffic to the site. So you see what I mean when I say that your site and you products are not businesses; your list is.

Step - 3 Market a Related Product

When you have built your list, nurtured it, cultivated that list, and have made those people on your list your friends then you can market any product to them. It is called Affiliate Marketing. This is where the monetization takes place. Affiliate Marketing is no doubt a multi-billion-dollar a year industry.

To achieve this, you will send a unique link to your list that directs them to the product that you know will be useful and of interest to them. If anybody clicks on the link and buys the product that you recommend then you make a commission on that product.

There are lots of places online that you can find products that will match the kind of niche you are in. Later on, you might even want to take it a bit further if you really enjoy that type of marketing and create your own product, then you can keep 100% of the profits if you choose not to use affiliates to sell it.

I would also like to mention that each of these steps has some elements attached to it. I will be suggesting a place where you can get the best information and private coaching if you so desire.

One golden rule you mustn't break is, "Never abuse your list". This is true because at the other end of your list are real people just like you and me. Real people with feelings, fears, and aspirations so you can bet they will respond in kind to the way you treat them. Most beginners always make the mistake of seeing dollar signs the moment they hear the word list so try not to have that notion in the beginning. Take time to create a relationship with your list, give value first and, if possible, over deliver on the value aspect. Once you've done this and your list has come to know and trust you then, and only then, can you market to them any related products.

THE TOOLS

Actually, when you set out to make money online, you will need some tools at your disposal. Unlike what you hear and see on the net, there is a certain amount of money that is involved in starting a business. Most of the time, people will tell you that you can make money without spending a dollar, but those types of businesses are few and far in between.

There are just three costs that involve three tools you simply cannot do without if you are really serious about creating a lasting business that puts money into your pocket. Whether you are there or not, sleeping or working on it, these tools are relatively very cheap and are items that selling a few affiliate products can pay for each month. These tools are:

1. A domain name. A domain name is the name of you website (such as ***easyimreviews.com***), or you can call it your online business address. This will cost between $5 to $10 a year.
2. Hosting. You will also need to host that domain name. This is what keeps your site online; without it, you simply have no business. The cost of this varies depending on the company offering the hosting services and what you as a customer want. But, all in all, you can get hosting between $7 to a few hundred dollars per month. Not to worry; I will show you a place where you can get free hosting for as many websites as you want for life.
3. Auto Responder. Do you remember when I was talking about list building? Good! Auto Responders help you to manage that list. With the help of auto responders, you can communicate with your list. This is an absolute must; there are no two ways

about it. The auto responder I use is called Aweber. The company is reliable. You can get registered for just $1 for the first month then not more than $20 every other month. As I said before, this payment can be taken care of by the sale of just a few products to your list.

As you can see, these three tools are very inexpensive, and they are tools that you simply can't avoid.

CHAPTER THIRTEEN

BEFORE YOU QUIT YOUR JOB..... FOR PETE'S SAKE!!

The trouble with unemployment is that the minute you wake up in the morning, you're on the job.-SLAPPY WHITE (Quoted in The Mammoth Book of Zingers, Quips, and One-Liners)

If you've got a J.O.B., you are already in the J.O.B.; there is no need to quit just yet because if you do, you just might regret it. Contrary to what most people think, you still need to have a roof over your head and food on your table. It's even more critical if you have a family to feed; that's even more reason you don't just quit your job yet.

If you are anything like me, I have come to cherish Fridays with a passion and loath Monday mornings with a passion. The following is a kind of cyclical pattern of those who seek to quite their day J.O.B.

Monday mornings have come to be, for most people (myself included), a dreaded moment. You are startled out of your sweet sleep by the blare of the alarm, then you hit snooze only for it to blast off again 5 minutes later, then you reluctantly drag yourself out of the bed and into the shower, still rubbing your eyes half asleep.

It's a way of life for lots of people who are tied to their jobs, struggling day in and day out, year after year, getting depressed more and more, and finding it hard just to put food on the table. They hate what they do; yet, they just can't stop. Why? Because the moment they stop, the money stops coming as well. It's a rat race, and the worst thing is most people won't be able to get out of that rat race until the day they breathe their last breath.

AND THEN THE SPARK!

In a typical night the stars are shining, and it's warm and cozy, but you can't eat nor sleep because you are so livid with anger: your boss had a rough day at home with his wife and took out his anger and frustration on you because you gave him the chance when you turned in that report late. So you decide to check out that website that your coworker said he came across the other day that offers to teach you how to make money online so you can quit your day job in a matter of weeks, and everything looks so good, genuine, and easy.

The website shows you all the people who have made it with their system in a couple of weeks and their fat bank balances. They also tell you that you have got **a sixty day money back guarantee!** You ask yourself: how much better could it get? If it doesn't work, I will have my money back so why not? It's so easy, and the money is chicken change.

So the next morning you hand in your resignation letter, give your boss the finger when his back is turned, walk out of his office, and out of J.O.B. You feel so free and happy because at last you are no longer a slave to some job. After all, making money online should be easy, just as they said on that website right?

REALITY

Wrong!! While it is possible to make money immediately, you still have to work at it and give it some time, just like any other business venture offline. Nothing good comes easy they say, although sometimes with luck you can make it **"fast"**, but the worst thing anybody can do is to get into business and rely on luck to see him or her through.

The reality is that you can make it online and **fast** (note that emphasis again) compared to a traditional online business or franchise. Fast here doesn't mean it's an overnight success or you quickly throw together a website, put it out on the internet, and then roll over and go to sleep hoping that when you check your bank balance the following morning you will have so much money that you don't know what to do with it.

No way my friend, not at all; there is work involved. You have to put in the time required to learn the basics and then have a plan to get you from where you are to where you want to be.

MY NEAR MISTAKE

I almost fell victim to that way of thinking. I almost quit my J.O.B before I was ready. But thank goodness I am my father's son. If there is one thing I learned from him, it's that you have to work before you can eat. It's from him that I picked up that saying "Nothing good comes easy". Just think about it. Let's take food, for example. Before you can eat you have to get the money to buy your food, get the items to the kitchen, spend some time cooking and sweating, all before you can eat. Then when everything is finished cooking, you need to get it to the dining table and with your fork transfer the food from the plate to your mouth and finally you swallow, right? So suppose someone decides to do all that for you: get the money for you, do the cooking for you, and put the food in your mouth; you still have to make the effort of swallowing the food yourself, right? If they have to use a tube to get it down your throat, then you are nothing more than a vegetable.

So that's my point: no matter how easy anything or system you see online may seem, there is still some work involved and until you change that mentality and stop looking for a get rich overnight scheme, you are never going to make it online.

KEEP YOUR JOB, BUT PART TIME

My J.OB then was such that I could do pretty much anything I want. I can decide I am not working for a day or two. They only problem is for that day or two, there will be no incoming money into my pocket, so I will have to depend on what I have saved before then.

So please, please, before you quit your job, even if you hate it with a passion just like I did mine, **whatever you do: don't just stop yet! Not yet!!** Keep it on the side, part time, so you will have time to be working on your business gradually until you get to a point where your business is making a little over what you are getting at your day job. Even then still don't quit yet; keep your part time job and get some money saved up that will last you for a couple of months just in case anything goes wrong with your business before you are fully stabilized.

After all, you need to put food on the table and keep a roof over your head. There is one golden rule with quitting your job and going into business for yourself and that is: **Make sure you love what you are doing!** If you don't love what you are doing, chances are you won't put in the effort, time, and commitment that are needed to succeed in that business.

So please think it through before you decide to fire your boss; think how that kind of life will affect you and your family, and keep your job until you are able to get your business fully into gear.

CHAPTER FOURTEEN

HOW BADLY DO YOU WANT IT? PAYING THE PRICE

Price is what you pay. Value is what you get.-Warren Buffet (Investor)

You see, I've come to realize that for everything you do there is always a price tag attached to it. No matter what it is, positive or negative, you have to pay a certain price. Take for example if you are a smoker: you pay the price of lung disease or cancer; if you can drive very well, you paid the price to learn how to drive; if you are the CEO of an organization, you paid the price of learning how to run an organization and earned the right for you to be trusted and given that position; if the company is yours then... you get what I mean.

The same goes for anyone who is seeking ways to make money online or offline for that matter. If anyone tells you that to make money online all you need to do is to get online and browse to your heart's content and at the end of the day your bank account will be full to the busting point then that person must be a joker. I am serious because if you stop to think about it for a minute, that's exactly how most of these products being thrown around on the Internet sound to me. Every product out there is the "best" as far as the marketer is concerned; the producer of the product will give a better reason why his product is simply the "best" you can get your hands on.

Making money online, like every other thing on earth that is worthwhile, takes patience, determination, perseverance, sharp eyes, and keen ears. Then, of course, you must be willing to pay the price. You have to sit down and do your checks and balances. Ask yourself what you want to achieve online and then find out what it takes to get there. You also need to know what you are willing to give up to get there. More often than not, you will find the price you need to pay, within and around those things, and what it will take you to go from where you are to wherever you are going when it comes to making money online. If you have got a family that does not understand, especially if you have never made a cent, then you have got a bigger problem. But, then, you can use the negativity to your advantage: prove them wrong and make it happen; not only will they be happy, but you will equally feel a deep sense of satisfaction and accomplishment.

CHAPTER FIFTEEN

AND FINALLY

Robert Kiyosaki once said "The rich build systems, while everybody else looks for work".

Most people's reaction to this book will be defensive; believe me, that's part of the conditioning. You can deny it all you want, but the truth remains that the cage you decided to put yourself in is still there. If this book didn't evoke any kind of emotion within you, then you are truly dead as far as financial freedom is concerned.

But if you got mad then that's a good thing; it shows that you still have some humanity left in you and that you can do whatever it takes to break free from the mold. You have to let the anger go through you and lead you to take those steps of courage. This will help you to start unlearning all that you have been forced to believe is true. You will get to do something about your situation and deal with all those years of negative conditioning.

Fear is one of the greatest things that hold people back from being who they are meant to be. Fear makes them live a mediocre life; it makes people live a domesticated lifestyle, like trained pets instead of living as the powerful human beings they were meant to be.

Another fear that most people encounter is the fear that they might not have any value to offer others, but this is misguided especially when you have not even tried at all. Every human has the ability to provide some form of value to others.

You might be doing it at your so-called J.O.B. without even realizing it but the moment you make that conscious effort and stop thinking like an employee then you will see the light and realize the potential locked inside of you.

All you will ever need is the ability to realize who you are, who you are meant to be, and your uniqueness in this beautiful world we live in. You just have to let you be you, express your real self to the world, start with those around you and expand from there. The human psyche is such that you can never know true happiness until you start living your real life.

Will Smith said to his son, "Don't let anybody say to you that you can't do something". Most of the time that they say something like that it is because they are afraid that you just might succeed. Sometimes they say it because they are afraid to try it themselves or they say it because they can't do those things themselves. Whichever it is, never pay attention. I always have this notion that there is no point in listening or paying attention to people who I know have no positive impact on my life or my goals, especially if they are being negative. This may sound a bit arrogant, but that's just me.

It's funny how people will whine and complain about problems they are facing in their J.O.B.s. Most of the time, the conditioning has made them so dumb and numb that they feel they are powerless to do something, so they vent their anger and frustrations on their boss or coworker (behind their backs of course). Sometimes they take those frustrations and anger back home and pour it all on their spouse and family. No wonder most families break up under such conditions. Such people living life under such conditions are simply cowards. They turned themselves into cowards the moment they felt they had no choice but to take whatever it was their boss threw at them and said, "Sorry, sir" at the same time.

Granted, it's not really easy to build a business or design

and implement your own money generating system. It takes some upfront work. Most of the time, you can hammer at it for months on end or even a year or two before you start making any headway at all. But you don't have to reinvent the wheel; there are lots of systems that have been created, tested, and debugged by people just like you. Nobody is born knowing it all; those guys had to learn the systems just as you will need to learn them as well. Simply pick one system and run with it. How long this takes you is irrelevant as you are aware the time will pass anyway. I think it's better you emerge sometime in the future as the owner of a proven system that generates income as opposed to continuing to live a life of self-servitude.

And there has never been a better time to start your own business than right now. Even if the statistics show that most business will fail before their fifth year I still think it's more fulfilling to try than to not try at all. Besides, in case you have forgotten, this is the information age where all you need to make your dreams come true is at your fingertips, and I mean that literally.

If you take a step back and ask yourself what lifestyle would you prefer: the knowledge and experience of working in a J.O.B. for 40 years or the knowledge of learning how to create systems that generate income for you whether you are working or not endlessly for years to come which would you choose? Well, I don't know about you but as for me, I would like the latter very much.

So what will it be? Would you prefer to be caged into a lifelong domestication system called J.O.B. what about the obedience training?, would you prefer to be rewarded by your master when you behave well and be punished when you make mistakes and fail to obey your master's commandments? Is there any atom of free will left inside of you or has your J.O.B. mentality so conditioned you to accept being a pet for life? It's amazing how deep social conditioning can run in some people's lives. It makes otherwise smart people believe the exact opposite of what the truth actually is.

While I don't think starting an online business is for everyone, the basic truth is that it's one of the best ways to generate income without needing a J.O.B. Most people simply love being employees, but the moment you are no longer happy with your J.O.B., then it's time to reconsider and start your own online business so you can start to actually live.

Much of what you've just read might sound condescending and arrogant to you. Well, I don't mean to sound like I have my head up my ..... Well you know. The thing is; I just want you to start thinking differently about you and the people around you. The way you leave your life now, is it what you want? Ultimately, the choice is yours to make.

Thank You

I sincerely have to say thank you for taking the time to buy and read this book and for sticking with me this long. Am not a native English speaker but at least I try, you have to give me that. I apologize for any errors or omissions found herein, so I will love to use this chance to ask for your feedback, anything at all that you think that I didn't do well or should have done better, please let me know. One thing I do know is that I don't know everything and I have room for growth but I can't do that with your help.

If this book struck a chord within you, if by any chance you can sincerely identify with anything said in this book then I know that I have at least achieved a measure of success so please take a moment to leave a review for this book. By going here on Amazon-

Leave A Review here

Your feedback and review will help me continue to write the kind of kindle book that will continue to give back and help people to find their way in these global economic crises.

And One Last Thing Before You Go Please………..

Kindle gives you the opportunity to rate and share your thoughts on FaceBook and Twitter.

If you believe this book is worth shearing, would you take a few seconds to let your friends and family know about it? Go ahead, post on FaceBook and Twitter. You never know it just might help somebody who is out of job to start thinking differently and start making a change in their lives. If anything, with the global financial crises, we need more entrepreneurs creating and building businesses rather than J.O.B seekers.

ONCE AGAIN, YOUR FREE GIFT,

I would like to remind you to go to

https://www.easyimreviews.com/resources/

For all the FREE GIFTS I promised you earlier.

Remember, BIGGY said it best *"you can't change the world till you change yourself"*

Please, if would take a few minutes to connect with me that will be awesome

FACEBOOK PROFILE: fb.me/EasyIMReviews

FACEBOOK PAGE: https://www.facebook.com/EasyIMReviews/

TWITTER PAGE: https://twitter.com/EasyIMReviews1

Excerpts from My Book "Virtual Real Estate Investing"

BRIEF HISTORY OF DOMAIN NAMES

As we know perfectly well, the arrival of the internet has been one of the greatest revolutions for humanity. This has changed the way of life for us all. Lifestyles change that includes, our interaction with one another, habits, and the way we do business. Every single aspect of our life has been impacted one way or another.

It's safe to say that work also has been impacted drastically. This has led to new opportunities and at the same time other professions obsolete.

The first domain was **www.symbolics.com** and it is therefore the oldest site in the world. The domain was purchased by the computer company Symbolics Inc, originally known as the Massachusetts-based Symbolics Computer Corporation, best known for making and distributing Personal Computers on a large scale.

In 2009, however, Aron Meystedt of XF.com, an investment company from Missouri, purchased the company and, therefore, also the domain.; the site is still active today and has become a sort of digital museum where users can retrace the infinite stages of the growth of the network from 1985 until today.

In addition to the www.symbolics.com website, 1985 saw the registration of only 5 other domains. A truly negligible number compared to the thousands of recordings that flood the various registrars around the world every day.

The millionth domain was registered as early as 1997.

As we can easily guess today, there are millions of domains scattered around on the internet.

Domain name syntax

A domain name is divided into two parts technically called labels, that are conventionally concatenated, and delimited by dots, such as example.com. That's according to Wikipedia. Such as- **example.com**.

The end of the "example.com" is referred to as Top-Level-Domain. "**.com**"

In 1985 there were only nine options to choose from: the first was **.com**, among others there were **.gov**, **.net**, **org**. And others like **.us**, **.uk** and **.il**, that is, the United States, England, and Israel, at the forefront. Although England has preferred to use a supra-domain before.UK, that is, co.uk, (where **.co** stands for commercial) but also, **.ltd.uk**, or **.gov.uk**. Other countries such as France, Germany, South Korea will come, together with others in 1986.

The birth of the internet is before 1985 and dates back to the 1960s. In those years, the USA developed a new defense and counter-espionage system. However, the invention of the domain name system (Domain Name System, DNS) gave the decisive push to the public to start using the network. It is a system used to assign names to hosts, or the "nodes" of the network within which the information is kept.

These names are useful for identifying the site the user is looking for. Without them, the search should take place through IP addresses, very complex numeric labels that uniquely identify network devices. The assignment of a name that is easily recognizable and memorable was, therefore, the key to facilitating the mass use of the greatest invention of the last century.

WHAT IS DOMAIN NAME INVESTING?

Domainers or Domain Investors, register domain names based on apparently generic phrases or words in the hope that these domain names may later be sold to businesses or end-users.

The purpose of a domainer is to buy the domains that he considers interesting, and that he can sell and make a profit from. If someone wants to develop a business linked to one of these domains, they will be ready to pay the price requested to obtain the right to use it.

In the United States, this is an old trade like the internet, and this kind of trade in domain names is highly developed and highly equipped.

Competition is very high. So, you need to choose domain names that you think you can resell and make a profit on.

The goal is to be the first to buy a domain that is not yet reserved, and which you think someone will need one day. Except that nothing says it will be exciting. So, buy sparingly, because you will keep your domains for months or even years.

The most representative domains are the domains linked to a generic activity (technology, decorations, games, fashion, etc.), as well as the brands of products that do not yet exist. But, since names in these areas have already been purchased, for the most part, you have little chance of finding the name that will be profitable.

The **domain trading business** is a tough one. It starts with small earnings, which you will improve over time. After at least 6 months, you should be able to earn something substantial. With the practice and the experience gained, you could over time turn it into a profitable business. And all this with only a few hours of daily work.

The domain trading is like investing in the stock market: you need to have a portfolio to limit risks and optimize earnings. Beginner domainers start with dozens of domains but begin to get serious from 50 domains. The professionals revolve around 150-300 domains.

Like any investment, domain names come with some risks. However, for diligent investors who consider risks and returns in-depth, domain names can become an investment that produces high returns.

MISTAKES TO AVOID WHEN SELLING YOUR DOMAIN NAME

Typossquatting-

If you want to go into domain trading, you must certainly be able to choose the right domain names but also avoid making some mistakes that newbies make when they are just starting.

The domain name that you will want to buy must be as original as possible and never a long word, but short enough to be easily remembered, these two assumptions are very important in this work and to create interest in buyers and increase the chances of success.

Forget the practice of registering domains with by practicing typossquatting. Typosquatting, also known as URL hijacking, is a form of cybersquatting (sitting on sites under someone else's brand or copyright) that targets Internet users who incorrectly type a website address into their web browser (e.g., "Gooogle.com" instead of "Google.com").

Apart from the fact that if you highjack a registered trademark; you run the risk of being sued but also it's kind of an expensive way to do **domain name trading** business. Besides, people who make mistakes when typing domain names are very few.

The two-letter reversal, the wrong domain extension, or a forgotten dash in the domain name is enough for a user to end up on the wrong website. The most popular websites are constantly attacked by typosquatters.

These speculate on the carelessness of users: when they enter a wrong URL they end up on websites containing advertisements, viruses, if not downright bogus pages, where you can be the victim of real scams or phishing attacks.

Typosquatters can end up in serious trouble with the law because, very often, registering a domain containing an error still violates the trademark right.

Since proceeding legally can prove to be a long and expensive process, it is always advisable to try to prevent this type of situation.

Many trademark owners use the strategy of simultaneously registering several possible domain variations with typos to protect themselves from competition or typosquatters. Website operators who use an easy-to-miss domain name should also consider logging variants with the most common errors. Once registered, domains with typos can be easily redirected via a redirect to your website.

To avoid Cybersquatting consists in registering or using a web domain in bad faith, to try to obtain an economic gain from registered trademarks and business.

Cybersquatters get most of their earnings by reselling these domains to those who own the rights to the exploited signatures.

Domain Discussion Forums

Forums on the web are sites where you can freely discuss topics that are focused on a particular niche. They have long been a part of the internet and the internet is home to thousands of them, and you can find them easily.

Many of them cover all kinds of topics where questions can be asked and answers found; others concern very specific topics such as "Domain Forums", where the main topic is domain names and all that concern a web domain. You can ask questions and wait for a plausible answer to your question or interact with other users by answering their questions.

Users and experts meet and discuss ideas, problems, or simply clarifications issues they might have.

Expiring Domains

When you decide to buy or sell a web domain, you are speaking improperly in the sense that buying or selling is not exactly the right words to use.

In reality, when we "buy" a web domain we are simply "renting" the use that you can generally decide for a year or 10. For the period in which you have rented it, it is as if it were yours and you can do whatever you want to do with it. You can decide to hold it or sell it if you want.

Being a rental and not a real purchase, the web domain in question will come to have an expiration date and you can decide whether to renew the use for a certain amount of time or leave it "free" knowing that someone else could re-rent it after you.

In the search for the best domain name, a completely wide

ecosystem of business has emerged and it will keep evolving. This ecosystem is made up of expired domain sites to be auctioned. There are ingenious systems to beat the competition overtime when a domain is released, domain reservations expiring, advice on the value and potential of a domain, and much more.

Drop Catching Services and Back Ordering Services

"The domain dropcatch, also known as the domain back-order, is the mechanism that allows you to register a domain name once the registration has expired, immediately after the expiry."

To understand how it works we must also know the "life cycle" of the web domain.

During the "grace period", the domains can be renewed from the panel that is made available by the registrar to the customer.

When this period is reached the domain will not resolve the DNS servers and therefore will stop working.

If you renew your domain during this period, it will work normally after a few hours.

If you have not renewed the domain and the grace period has expired, the redemption phase will pass.

"The redemption period" is the period in which the domain cannot be renewed in the usual way, this is because the domain is not renewable and must be recovered. The cost of this recovery is higher than the usual renewal price.

To renew a domain that is in the Redemption Period, the renewal price is usually at least double the registration price (sometimes even much more)

If you have requested domain recovery, this procedure takes a few moments (after paying). Once it's active you have to wait a few hours.

If you decide not to recover it, the domain will go to the next state: "Pending Delete".

Upon reaching this state, the domain cannot be renewed because it is waiting to be removed from the registry. The next phase is that of "droptime", the domain can, therefore, be regained.

About forty-eight hours before the release, lists of domain names in droptime will be published on the main domain back-order platforms, so that customers and interested people can see them.

If there is a domain name in the list that interests you, you can try to book it through one of the backorder platforms.

If you don't want to use one of these platforms, you can try to register it manually after the droptime. The greater the interest in a domain, the less likely it is to be able to register it by hand.

TOOLS TO FIND NEW DOMAINS

Many websites on the internet allow you to "buy" a domain as there are other sites or tools that help us find new domains or better ideas regarding the name as a touch of originality never hurts.

"Namemesh" is a very interesting tool for discovering new ideas thanks to a wide range of customizations to be included in the name searches. There is a lot of information that you get just from the search results of this tool. Also, there is the possibility to decide which extensions to show with a simple click. Namemesh makes it easy to find good **SEO** friendly URL combinations.

If the keyword you were aiming for is already taken, you can try typing it in the "Lean Domain Search" search bar and you will have other suggestions that are close to what you want. For those who do not have enough ideas, for those seeking inspiration or for anyone wondering how to choose the right domain.

With "Bust a Name" an interesting solution is offered, just type two words, press enter and a large list of combinations and very interesting alternatives will appear. This helps you find original names. An excellent tool for the undecided, for bloggers who do not have clear ideas of what they want for a domain name. Or simply one who is looking for something new or simply to have a starting point on which to base themselves.

With "Instant domain search" just type a word and you will have a list of all the solutions, the free ones, and those already engaged. The Whois allows you to discover the owners and the suggestions' column gives you good advice for the alternatives in the domain choice.

Still "wordoid.com" and "Dot-o-motor" are two other valid alternatives.

DOMAIN APPRAISING SERVICES

Evaluating a domain or website is an estimate that takes into account numerous factors and can also be carried out with the help of online tools or expert advice.

Using domain brokers is perhaps the most reliable way to get an accurate estimate of the value of your domain.

There are also numerous online tools and software such as "Estibot.com" that allow you to estimate the value of a website or internet domain for free and immediately.

However, this software gives a very different and not very objective estimate, based on parameters which are not related to the US reference market.

Another alternative is the online forums that allow you to have a non-automatic but free web domain evaluation. Also, the evaluation is not done by robots but by individuals who have certainly gained experience in the sector.

Domain Aftermarket Auction House

The buying and selling of web domains through auctions is a constantly growing market. This is of interest both for those looking for a particular domain to associate with specific web activity and for those who want to build a new profession, exploring the opportunities of speculation that this sector can offer.

When you want to register a domain, the advice is to visit sites for domain auctions: **Afternic**, **SnapNAMES**, and **GoDaddy** are just some of the most famous.

Once the auction site has been chosen, it will be possible to (try to) register a domain or choose between expiring and auctioned domains. However, the actual value of the domain must be carefully evaluated: the domains with a high value are the short ones because they can be easily memorized, those containing keywords and those with a good "**SEO**". Websites such as "**Namebio**" allow you to collect sales information about a particular keyword and, consequently, to quantify the value of a domain containing that keyword.

After the necessary analyzes and after determining the available budget, it will be possible to make an offer for a domain or, when possible, to deal directly with the owner.

If, on the other hand, the goal is to sell a domain, after having evaluated it with the aforementioned tools, you can rely on sites such as "Escrow" to manage the transactions and the transfer of the domain itself.

Registrars

The registrar could be called "a broker".

Registrars have accredited companies that, in collaboration with the registry, deal with the sale and assignment of domain names, and manage them on behalf of their users.

Registrars also often offer other Internet-related services such as **hosting**, mailboxes, DNS management up to the creation of websites. After demonstrating that they possess the requirements, the registrars enter into a contract with the registry, to which they pay a monthly or annual fee, ensuring them certain guarantees in the management and resale of the domain names. Once the authorization to sell a domain name has been obtained, the registrar will choose independently not only the services to be offered, but also the costs for registration and any maintenance.

There are many on the web, sometimes impossible to choose one all with different prices and offers.

Certainly, some of the best known and most popular are: **NameCheap**,

Bluehost Domains, **Google Domains**, **Register.com**, **Hostinger**, **HostGator**, **Domain.com**.

DOMAIN MARKETPLACES

There are also several marketplaces dedicated to the sale of web domains, just as there are also marketplaces that sell everything and where domains can be sold. Websites focused on selling products where supply and demand meet.

There is an infinite number of them since the internet is now able to offer anything and, in every area, there is a lot of competition, so it is also for marketplaces.

The most famous, known and appreciated are certainly:

Buydomains.com- an excellent site worldwide that offers millions of domains for sale and which focuses mainly on "Premium" domains. By typing any keyword, all the related words will appear with the sale price, and you can also do an offer and negotiate with the price, an excellent site therefore also for those wishing to sell their web domain, and therefore looking for reliable customers, looking for the best.

Namecheap- One of the popular marketplaces. A marketplace is highly known and used by the most enterprising **internet marketers** who are looking for opportunities both in the sale and in the purchase. Through the search engine of the site, you can find the domain that most interests, and make an offer;

Domain.com- Another great alternative for our business.

This marketplace also offers different domain options, favoring "Premium" ones

Igloo- Another popular and beautiful site that offers domains in different markets, and of all types, including "Premium". It gives you all the necessary tools and information to meet your domain business needs. Igloo also offers several and beautiful custom templates that make it easier for you to negotiate online on the platform.

Fortunately, the internet today has made it possible for many to get involved and cave out a niche for themselves. Entering the business of selling web domains is one of the options that are available to anyone willing to put in the work.

Investing in websites is a process that allows any savvy user to make a sizable profit. The process should be three-fold: invest in flipping, parking, and developing websites. The better you can do at this, the more likely it is for your business to do very well, without a lot of long-term commitment.

Consider the different ways to invest in domain investing, or website investing.

1. **Invest in website flipping:**
   Here, you will purchase a domain name and start to develop the website. Once you have some level of secure footing, you then sell the website at a profit.

2. **Invest in domain name parking:**
   Here, the website owner registers a domain name. Then, with very little cost, they do nothing more than sit on it and try to sell it to those that may be interested in buying it.

3. **Invest in website development:**
   Purchase a domain name, work to establish the website, and then hold on to it and profit from it.

In each of these situations, there is profit to be had. Domain name parking offers the lowest potential returns unless you have a very high demand for this type of domain name that a company feels they must have. Investing in a website and then flipping it is a great way to turn a profit, especially if you know how to set up a website fairly quickly and what it takes to get the **Internet marketing** going on it. Finally, owning and **developing a website** is the largest profit maker because the long-term benefits far outweigh the short term selling in either of the two prior options.

Yet, the profits may be well off into the future.

Some **Internet marketers** use all of these methods and they do so very successfully. As your business grows, you too can make decisions later about how you use it. For example, you may find that you purchased a domain name and build a website you planned to own and run for some time. But, in a few months, the website is going strong and in turn, you have an offer to buy it that you simply could not refuse.

In all scenarios, the goal is to find and secure a website that will work for your goals. The development of that website hinges on the same factors as any other would.

You'll need to develop a website that offers good information, good keywords, and is an attractive domain name. Depending on the extent of your goals with that domain name, you'll want to build a successful website that people will want to own.

In this book, we'll take a look at what each of these areas can offer to you. We'll also talk about how to get started in each one. For many Internet marketers, even those that are just **starting**, these are the foundations of success in their business. This is how they make a sizable amount of money month after month.

DOMAIN NAME PARKING

The first and simplest form of making money from website investing is through domain name parking. Here, you can invest very little, usually just a few dollars. When you park a domain name, you simply secure the domain's use for another time's use. It can also be done to redirect traffic or for resale.

For example, perhaps you have come up with a fantastic website name and you wish to hold on to it before anyone else can snatch it from you. To do this, you simply purchase the domain name and it will sit there, usually with an "Under Construction" page up. The site may also be, "Coming Soon..." There is no deadline for developing the website. There is only the cost of renewing the domain name each year.

Those who determine they want to keep the domain name after the first year can renew it and start developing the website. This is a great way to finally get your website up and serving your purpose. You will then need to pay for hosting of the website at the point when you will develop it. This will include purchasing enough space for the site. At the time the website has hosting, it no longer is a parked website.

On the other hand, you may find it helpful to use it as a redirection page. For example, if you have a Yourname.com domain name, you may also want to purchase a Yourname.net domain name. Then, use the second page to direct traffic to the first page, in case people type in the wrong address into their navigation bar.

To make a profit selling a website, you may also want to consider domain parking. In this instance, you will park the website to simply hold on to the domain name. For instance, perhaps you have come up with a fantastic domain name you know a company may want at some point. You purchase it and park the website (meaning you don't even pay for website hosting for it.)

Then, you resell the domain name (at a sizable price, of course) and make a profit from it. It was very common for Internet marketers to do this type of transaction back in the early years of domain names, but it still holds today. Many businesses use this method as a method of increasing profits solely based on keywords and niche topics.

COMPARING IT TO REAL ESTATE

How does domain name parking make you money? Compare how it would work in a general real estate transaction.

With domain name parking, you are simply purchasing the land that someone may need at some point. For example, there may be a field out nowhere, in particular, that is open, filled with grass and rolling hills. Right now, it does not do much and doesn't have a lot of value. But, you notice it is just a few miles from a developing city. By purchasing it now, when the price is low for it, you can resell it later at a higher price simply because you were in the right place at the right time.

Domain name parking is quite similar. There is very little to invest in, just in purchasing the domain name. There is also very little to do with the website once you purchase it except hold on to it. Some Internet marketers will use it for Adsense, or other advertising, but unless the site does get a lot of traffic (especially if the traffic is not consistent) likely, it won't rack in too much money.

Turning A Profit

How can you turn a profit with domain name parking?

- Know who would want to purchase this domain name. Why would this name be a good choice down the road? Keywords, similarity to another, larger website, or some other reason?

- Determine if the domain name parking is the best recourse. Would it be better to further develop the website and then sell it? You'll find more on this in just a bit.

- Market the purchase of the domain name, alerting those who may be on your mailing list or otherwise involved in the niche that you have the domain name available. Many will consider it.

- Use keywords and a catchy phrase to attract interested

parties. Think, what would someone in this niche be interested in?

- Hold on to it and watch the value grow. If you aren't in a rush, you may want to hold on to the domain name in a developing niche and sell it later when the value may be higher.

While domain name0 investing is a good option for many, it is not necessarily the only option. You should also be considering the other options you have with website investing, namely how you can make even more money from the purchase of it.

WEBSITE FLIPPING

Website flipping is the next step up in website investing. In this instance, you are moving one step forward: investing in a domain name, hosting the website, and getting the website up and running.

The best way to look at website flipping is to compare it to a real estate transaction: house flipping. With a home, you purchase the property at a low price. In this case, the website is virtually nothing. You may purchase a website already in place and improve it. Or, you can select a website domain name and start building from scratch.

The cost is again very small initially. Once you have the website under your control, you add to it, increasing its value just as a home investor would invest enough money to get the house in a higher-valued condition. They often modernize it, changing out any necessary appliances, and often repair the damage. By investing $20,000 to $30,000 into the home (not the website!) they wind up making a substantially larger return on their investment, perhaps even doubling the value of the property.

The same is true with website flipping. You come in with a very low price, build up the value of the website, and then sell it to someone (or a company) that can further carry it to success. The profit potential here is unlimited, depending on the niche and the overall success of the website you design.

Additionally, website flipping is not just about turning a small profit on getting a website started. It is also the process of finding underperforming websites, purchase the website, and increase the value of it. Then, you turn around and sell it for a larger profit. The fact is, many businesses online are still very new and they are often far less profitable than they could be.

To be successful at website flipping, you simply must know how to build a website with success. The more traffic it gets, the revenue it brings in overall high quality of the website will define if the website is worth more, and therefore if anyone will invest in it.

Advantages of Buying an Expired Website\Domain

There are some advantages to purchasing a website that already has been established, improving it, and then selling it off. For example, these websites already have an established audience. This means you do not have to develop an audience yourself. This could help you turn a real profit right away, simply by improving the search engine optimization of it or by installing an improved Adsense campaign, for example.

In addition to this, the website is likely already indexed in search engines. This is a fantastic tool because the website's ability to make a profit is likely to happen much faster. This can mean getting into the top search results faster. Even websites with very little attention likely have some type of backlink network already developed for it.

Another benefit of purchasing a website already developed is as simple as avoiding the Google Sandbox. This is only possible if you purchase a website that has made it through the first 12 months of life.

How To Buy A Website

Let's assume you will be purchasing a website that you want to **develop and flip**. It has already been in place for some time, and you know it is likely to be a great investment for your business. First off, you need to realize what the site can do for you and how it will fit in the strategy you are developing for your business.

You may wish to purchase a website that is already getting targeted traffic for the product or service that you are already promoting. By purchasing a website like this, you can then take all the traffic that is already going there and funnel it to your products and sales pages. For this to work well for your business, do be sure that the traffic coming to the website is high enough to warrant the purchase and quality enough to help turn a profit. High traffic does not mean you are getting good traffic. In the next section, we will talk more about purchasing a website and expanding and developing it.

On the other hand, you may just want to purchase the website and flip it. In this situation, you have to look for the right website to purchase. As a house flipper knows, it is more than just knowing what the actual problems are with the house. You also need to know the market for the house, or in this case, the website.

There is a risk in purchasing a website for the sole reason of flipping it. It can be very costly to make a mistake since you will likely be investing a good amount of money into the flip. In this situation, you need to ensure that you purchase websites that have the highest profit potential. You need to see a large result from the time and money you put into the site to make it worthwhile. On top of this, you also need to be sure that there is a market for purchasing it after you have created the final, finished copy.

Some of the best websites for this are underperforming **e-commerce websites** that are selling a product. The product they are selling should be in a well-established market. Look for a market that may be just starting to take off. In addition to this, be sure that the website itself has potential. For example, if it already has great search engine optimization, chances are good it may not get much better. Of course, the website's owners have to be willing to sell.

To make a profit from flipping websites, you have to master the following:

- Choose the proper website that can provide you with the likely potential sale you are hoping for.

- Implement changes quickly. This usually includes making a few changes to see a significant increase in the functioning and profitability of the website, in multiple areas.

- Get a double-digit increase in sales for the website, a sure sign the website is profitable.

- Get the work done and working for you before the general marketplace gets caught up to you.

- Do this and you can make a sizable profit on the website by selling it for a premium.

- Don't wait so long that the Internet is saturated with those who are selling the product or service you are.

It is important to remember that the Internet is one of the fastest moving marketplaces anywhere. The competitiveness of the web is also just as fast-moving. To buy and flip websites with success, you will need to know what to do, how to do it, and get it done as soon as possible. You should also be up to date on the movement on the web, including the strategies helping the web to move fast.

Take into consideration this method of website investing carefully. It takes the combination of just the right scenario to make a profit. This method of investing is best for those who have experience in website development and profitable website design.

DISCLAIMER

While all attempts have been made to verify the information provided in this publication, neither the author nor the publisher assumes any responsibility for error, omissions, or contrary interpretations of the subject matter herein.

This book is purely for informational purposes only. The views expressed are those of the author alone, and should not be taken as expert instruction or commands. The reader is responsible for his or her actions.

Adherence to all applicable laws and regulations, including international, federal, state and local governing professional licensing, business practices, advertising, and all other aspects of doing business in the US, Canada or any other jurisdiction is the sole responsibility of the purchaser or reader.

Neither the author nor the publisher assumes any responsibility or liability whatsoever on the purchaser or reader of these materials.

Every effort has been made to accurately represent this book and its potential. Even though this industry is one of the few where one can write their own check in terms of earnings, there is no guarantee that you will earn any money using the techniques and ideas in these materials. Examples in these materials are not to be interpreted as a promise or guarantee of earnings. Earnings potential is entirely dependent on the person using our book, ideas and techniques. We do not purport this as a get rich quick scheme. Your level of success in attaining the results claimed in our materials depends on the time you devote to the knowledge and various skills. Since these factors differ according to individuals, we cannot guarantee your success or income level. Nor are we responsible for any of your actions.

The author and publisher do not warrant the performance,

effectiveness or applicability of any sites listed or linked to in this book. All links are for informational purposes only and are not warranted for content, accuracy or any other implied or explicit purpose.

Any perceived slight of any individual or organization is purely unintentional. As always, the advice of a competent legal, tax, accounting or other professional should be sought.

www.ingramcontent.com/pod-product-compliance
Lightning Source LLC
Chambersburg PA
CBHW060852220526
45466CB00003B/1338